Totally Me

The Teenage Girl's Survival Guide

Yvonne Collins and Sandy Rideout

Adams Media Corporation
Holbrook, Massachusetts

*First and foremost, thanks to Michelle, Amanda, Melissa, Jennifer
and their friends, who inspired the book and provided insights along the way.
Thanks also to Carolyn Swayze for her efforts on our behalf, to Paula Munier-Lee
for her advice and encouragement, and to Dawn Thompson for keeping us on track.
As always, we appreciate the support of our parents.
Special thanks to Dave for his enthusiasm and endless (we hope!) supply of good ideas.
Last, we thanks our friends, in the company of whom we remain "girls."*

❋ · ❋ · ❋

Published by
Adams Media Corporation
260 Center Street, Holbrook, MA 02343
www.adamsmedia.com

ISBN: 1-58062-410-3

Printed in Canada.

J I H G F E D C B A

Library of Congress Cataloging-in-Publication Data
available from printer.

*This book is available at quantity discounts for bulk purchases.
For information, call 1-800-872-5627.*

Contents

part two
They're Goofy, They're Gross, and Damn It, They're Great! Let's Talk About Boys / 37

* chapter eight *

Hot Lips / 83

* chapter nine *

So, You've Got a Boyfriend (This Week, Anyway) / 88

* chapter ten *

The Wild Thing / 95

* chapter eleven *

The Dump Truck: Is That You Behind the Wheel? / 106

✳ chapter sixteen ✳

Getting What You Want / 146

✳ chapter seventeen ✳

Quality Time / 163

✳ chapter eighteen ✳

Love and the Single Parent / 175

part four

Baby, You're the Greatest / 189

✳ chapter nineteen ✳

Yakkity Yak–Learn to Talk Back / 191

✳ chapter twenty ✳

Hormones: Your Evil Copilot / 202

✳ chapter twenty-one ✳

It's Your Body, You'd Better Get Used to It / 212

✳ chapter twenty-two ✳

Help! Who Am I? / 220

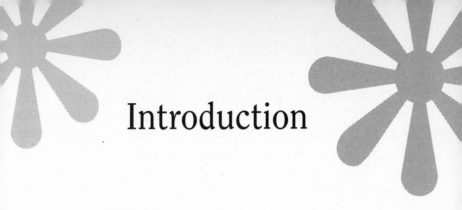

Introduction

Is your family driving you crazy?

Are you aching for more independence?

Are you fed up with listening to your best friend yammer on about her new boyfriend?

Are you fed up with not having a boyfriend to yammer on about?

Do you find yourself in a state of absolute rage one day and pure bliss the next?

Is frustration your best friend—and confusion your middle name?

*W*ell, read on, girlfriends, because the cavalry has arrived. We've been there, we've done that, and we know what you're going through.

Life as a teen is no picnic. Adulthood is coming at you like a monster truck picking up speed. You're making all kinds of new friends, and each one comes with her own set of rules. You're fascinated by boys, and each one comes with his own set of rules that no female can read. You're facing pressure from your peers, pressure from your parents, and most of all, pressure from yourself. It's enough to make the coolest girl's head explode!

In the midst of all this, you're trying to establish yourself as an individual and find your "signature style" (we're not just talking fashion here). That's the greatest challenge of the teen years. You want to stand out—but not too far. You want to be yourself—but only if everyone loves you. You want to try everything—but only if you won't make any mistakes.

It's exhausting yet strangely exhilarating. There are probably times you'd love to run to your parents for help in steering through this confusing minefield, but your need for independence stops you dead in your tracks. What's a girl to do?

That's where we come in. Although we can't wave a magic wand and make all the craziness disappear, we *can* help you understand some of the challenges you're facing. We've become masters of putting weirdness into perspective—and perspective is the key to all things. Once you've found it, you can take control and focus on the business of becoming your fabulous self.

So how did we become masters of perspective? We struggled in adolescence as much as anyone but we made it our mission to survive the turbulence with sense of humor intact. That accomplished, we went on to become professional observers of human nature. One of us does this on a film set, where she stands behind the camera. The other is a full-time writer. This means we get paid to watch and learn, and now we want to share our knowledge and advice with you. Don't worry, we tested it out on the teens in our lives first.

And trust us, this won't hurt a bit. Close your bedroom door, put on your favorite tunes, and chill out with this book. This is a lecture-free zone—and we definitely don't do nagging. What we will do is provide funny and helpful advice, quizzes, lists, and true stories from other teenage girls who face the same challenges you do.

First, we'll take a good look at friendship, the good times and the bad. Next, we'll dish out ALL the goods on boys—how to find 'em, how to catch 'em, and how to toss 'em back when it's time to move on. Then, we'll spend some time talking about parents—how to live peacefully with them, and maybe even convince them to give you a little more freedom. Finally, we'll look at some of the changes your mind and body are undergoing as you head out into the world to become . . . yourselves.

It's only the beginning of a long voyage of self-discovery. Along the way you're going to realize how wonderful you are. We already think so, or we wouldn't have bothered to write a book just for you!

part one

Thank God
for the Girls

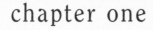

chapter one

Adventures in Chickland

She's at your house faster than a speeding bullet when you're feeling blue. She plows through your enemies more powerfully than a locomotive. She's able to leap tall desks at a single bound (to deliver your note to a cute guy). She's a bird. She's a dame. She's **Supergirlfriend.**

*I*f you've already met Supergirlfriend, you've struck gold and you probably know it. She's the one who can charm the crusty parent, the surly teacher, the obnoxious boy, and on a good day, even the most evil girl in your grade. You can take her anywhere because she knows just what's called for in any situation. She can create fun out of absolutely nothing. You look forward to her arrival and you are sorry to see her go, even if you've spent the entire day just talking about the complications of your lives. She's the confessor of your sins and champion of your triumphs. Who could live without her?

Almost any woman you know will tell you at length about the amazing talents of her friends. In the telling, she will become visibly proud and happy. It's as if she's laying her jewels out on the table for all to admire. She'll tell you that she doesn't see as much of them as she would like (because it's never enough), and that she always comes away from a visit ready to face the battle again. She has the satisfied look of a woman who has done all the upfront work of building great friendships and knows she will never be totally alone in the world. And that happiness, superfriends-in-training, can be yours too.

The Language of Friendship

Girlfriends always understand you. It seems like magic, but it's really just a matter of paying attention. They listen to you and they take the trouble to figure out how you think and feel. They learn all the tiny details that weave your intricate lives together. In short, they keep up, even when you're hurtling along at 200 miles per hour. What's most amazing is that supergirlfriends always know exactly what you mean, even if it's not what you *say*. They're masters of subtext, which is more than you can say for the rest of the people in your life.

Say the unthinkable happens: The guy you've been going out with steadily for three weeks is seen talking to the most beautiful girl in school—the one he worshiped from afar until you came on the scene. When you hear the horrible news, your world rocks on its axis. You know immediately that it signals the end for you and Lover Boy—and that everyone from the principal to the janitor has probably heard about it. It's the tragedy of your year so far.

You might try to explain what's happened to your parents, but it's quite possible that neither one will "get it." For one thing, you'll probably only give them fragments of the story and leave them to fill in the blanks (we know you, remember!). They're busy people who may not have the patience to read between the lines to discover why you're really upset. Although they're quite adept at grasping a concrete problem like "I'm failing math," when it comes to understanding the implications of "Ryan talked to Vanessa," they're easily confused.

You could go straight to your older sister, if you have one, and tell her your troubles. She'll probably rush you through your story, but she might give you some good advice, if she's in the mood. On the other hand, she has been known to get that superior "been there, done that" tone in her voice, as if the extra years she's had on this earth make all the difference. She may end up telling you straight out what you should do, whereas you're looking for help in figuring it out for yourself.

You might try to explain the tragedy to your brother, but there again you'll be doomed to disappointment. Guys have a completely different frame of reference and will likely focus on elements of the story that are not particularly helpful. For example, he might remind you how attractive Vanessa is so that you won't feel badly about your boyfriend lusting after her—every guy does! (Guys define this as sympathy, by the way.) Then perhaps he'll advise you to "just move on."

Your best girlfriend, however, will just know how you feel without your saying a word. In fact, before you've even called her, she's likely to show up on your doorstep with everything you'll need to get over the tragedy—junk food, a trashy magazine, and her favorite sweater for you to borrow. By the time you've talked it through for an hour or two, you'll decide you're better off without him.

The secret of girlfriend magic is that their experience of life is so similar to yours that they can completely relate to what you're facing each and every day. They know how you feel because they *feel* how you feel—and they say so in words that make sense. Somehow this convinces you that you are not alone and misunderstood. In fact, you have a social safety net!

It's in the Details

There's no cause too big or too small for the girls to take on. They'll ride two buses to the mall in the pouring rain to help you choose a new T-shirt to wear on your date. They'll keep you company on family trips or tag along for moral support when you need to approach a teacher for extra help. And if it's information about some new crush you need, you have your own army of spies. They'll find out more about that boy than a government agency ever could. Before the week's out, you'll know his favorite movie, whether he wears boxers or briefs, and why he broke up with his last girlfriend.

Oh yeah, they'll find out if he thinks you're cute, too. Mind you, if he doesn't, they won't likely tell you straight out. Good pals will rarely say something that will hurt you, even if you've asked for the information. Instead, you'll find the truth strategically buried in detail. Here's an example:

You: Did you talk to Connor?
She: Yeah, I caught him at his locker after school. I only had to walk by twice.
You: Did you find out if he's single?

She: Yah—but first I gotta tell you that Lena told me this morning that Connor wasn't very nice to his last girlfriend. He flirted with other girls when they were together.

You: Oh no! Really? That would kill me!

She: I know! And, I gotta tell you, he doesn't look as cute up close. I was surprised! His eyes are really small—sneaky-small, if you know what I mean.

You: Did you ask if he's seeing anyone?

She: Well, I think he kinda likes Carolyn.

You: Did he say that?

She: Not exactly. I just got that sense.

***She means**: He turned to watch Carolyn walk down the hall with **that look** on his face.*

You: Did you talk about me?

She: I didn't give any specifics. But you know, I don't think he's your type anyway.

You: I guess not. Not if Carolyn is, that's for sure.

***You mean**: My hopes are crushed, but at least he doesn't know I like him and besides, he isn't sounding like a prize.*

She: There are lots of fish in the sea—and some of them will have brains big enough to recognize how great you are!

Now, for the sake of comparison, here is how the same conversation might flow between two guys.

Connor: Did you ask Carolyn if she likes me?

Greg: Yah. She doesn't know you're alive, man. Sorry.

Notice that the guys communicated the same information using a fraction of the words. This is why they have so much time for sports and video games. They don't spend hours beating around the bush. The boys' conversation looks pretty brutal from a girl's point of view, but it is efficient. The girls understood each other perfectly and there were no hurt feelings. The same is true for the guys, who are able to toss off casual remarks to each other that would knock a girl to her knees. For example: "God, Greg, you're a hog. Look at the flubber on ya, man. You'd better stop stuffin' the cookies."

Well, whatever works for them . . . Give us face-saving diplomacy any day. We'll make the time! Besides, the exercise of learning to position a message carefully is excellent preparation for a career in just about any field—especially politics!

Analyze This

Girls develop this tactful and indirect style of relating through the exchange of large volumes of information and the painstaking analysis of everything that happens in the course of a day. Nothing is too trivial to share. That's partly because everything in life is much more fun when you share it with a girlfriend. Even boys. Especially boys. Of course, we don't mean that you would share the boy himself (not literally—well, unless you're into that sort of thing, Kinky Knickers), but half the fun of pursuing some new cutie is analyzing every last detail of the chase with your girlfriends. The only thing that comes close to matching the thrill of a good date is the full debrief with the girls afterward. No doubt you use that fabulous memory of yours, which is *so* wasted on history, to recall each and every detail of your encounters with that boy. Your friends will expect—and receive—an itemized report:

* What he wore
* What he said
* How good he smelled
* Whether he paid for your lunch, held your hand, or walked you home
* Where he rates on the smooch scale

And that's just for starters! Go on, admit it. Nothing is finer than hearing the sound of your own voice rambling on about the Boy of the Month. And the girls are so great. They'll tell you how cute he is and how nice he is and how lucky you are to have him. What's more, they'll be truly interested in:

* The color of his eyes
* His parents' first names
* Whether he wears button- or zip-fly jeans

✳ Whether he's a typical Libra

✳ Whether he snores (so he fell asleep during a chick flick—at least he went!)

Okay, so maybe they're not truly interested in *all* the details, but they'll fake it. Somehow they take everything in. They'll answer your e-mail, return your calls, and respond to every voicemail and page (even if you leave four back-to-back). You can't help but be amazed by their powers of retention. They can recall the precise phrasing of a sentence he uttered on your first date and haul it out four months later as Exhibit A. They're very clever girls, your friends.

And flexible, too, because when it all falls apart, they can turn on a dime and slag that boy off until there's nothing left of him but the lock of hair they managed to snip for you when he was distracted at a party. Of course, you'll still want to ramble on about him for hours and they'll listen, but now it's a Trash Fest. You'll list the rotten things he did and they'll help you remember. They'll point out how nerdy he's been looking lately, how dumb his jokes are, and how lucky you are to be rid of him. They'll laugh at his new haircut and the fact that he's been breaking out really badly since your breakup—from the stress, perhaps.

Then, when you turn around and like him again, they'll ignore your flip-flop and immediately "forget" those bad things and start noticing some improvement in him. His hair is growing out, his face is clearing up, and his sense of humor is improving, thank god. "It was just a bad phase," they'll say, "you're a good influence on him."

Girlfriends have to be very quick and very careful. After all, for teens, little is permanent—especially feelings about guys. Most girls develop "selective attention," meaning that we notice only what's appropriate for a given situation, dismiss what isn't, and suspend judgment. This allows us to support people completely while giving them plenty of room to move.

The Cheerleading Squad

Boys are no doubt a popular topic of discussion for you these days, but we know that's not all you're about. You're telling your girlfriends about your parents, your marks, and your problems with the clique at school, as well as your worries about the shape of your body and your overgrown eyebrows. Most important, you're confiding your dreams so they can help you try to figure out how to make them a reality. If your friends are all they should be, you'll be able to confess your darkest fears about the future to them, knowing they will spin things around so it doesn't look as scary.

What girlfriends do best, of course, is convince you that you're special. Deep down inside, we all want to believe we are, and we dream about finding a way to express this to the world. Maybe you're meant to be a rock star or poet or corporate head or astronaut and/or a great mom. There is some hidden talent that you sense but may not be able to put your finger on. The girls are so observant that they'll notice your gift *and* help you develop it. They'll encourage you to tell your best stories, or sing your heart out, or take your best slapshot.

Girlfriends don't even need proof of your talent to believe in it. Because they want to believe in their own promise, they're usually generous about believing in yours. They're your safety net, remember, so take courage and perform. Try acting out that scene or showing off your artwork. They will applaud every effort. Why wouldn't they? You're doing the same for them, right? One day you'll look around you and think, "How did I manage to hook up with this talented group?"

Estrogen Therapy

No one on this planet can find more to chat about than two teenage girls. The diversity and sheer volume of girltalk is stunning at any age, but at no time is our yakking more prolific than when we are teens. You know it's true. Boyfriends and parents will marvel at your stamina. They won't always understand that talking to your girlfriends is therapeutic. After all, parents and guys are often inclined to "solve" your problems for you. You want to solve them yourself. Girlfriends lend the sympathetic ear and fresh perspective that allow you to figure out your own solutions. Because they're an extension of you, their input doesn't feel like an intrusion.

Sharing your feelings with people you trust brings a wonderful feeling of relief, of course, but there is always a risk to confiding in others and most of us get burned at some point. You might get caught in that nasty game of "telephone." That's where you tell one person one thing and it migrates through a crowd and comes back as something far different—usually something hurtful or embarrassing.

Our mothers used to say, "If you don't have anything good to say, don't say anything at all." Please! Saying bad things is one of the great joys of friendship. We do acknowledge, however, that it's best to figure out if the people in whom you confide are trustworthy. So, until you know someone well, be cautious about what you share. Ask yourself, "Do I want the whole school to know this?" If the answer is no, keep your lips sealed.

The Golden Age of Friendship

You're entering the golden age of friendship. Over the next 10 years, you'll meet the friends you will keep your whole life. Now is the time to experiment—to test out friendships and see what works best for you. You'll learn a lot about relating to others in this process. It may look to the untrained eye as though you're just "hanging" with the girls, but what you're really doing is learning things from them that you no longer want to learn from your parents. Friendship is a fabulous training ground. Let's face it, parents can be irritating, and you probably tell them so frequently and at high volume. If you did that to your friends, it wouldn't take you very far. In their company, you have no choice but to learn how to be tactful, generous, loyal, supportive, and cooperative. Your parents might *tell* you how to behave in polite company, but your friends *show* you. Through trial and error, you discover how to make other people like you and want to spend time with you. Because you want to be liked, you figure it out. One day you look up and you've become civilized!

We are all shaped by our friendships, for better or worse. Obviously, it isn't a bad idea to look at your friends' credentials if you plan to give them this power over your life. Check out some of their other friends and see if they treat each other with respect. Have you put the responsibility for your training into capable hands? Choose well and you can become the girlfriend everyone covets. Choose badly and . . . well, we won't go there, because you won't! You've probably already chosen friends who are grooming you for greatness completely without pain.

Quiz

Which of the following statements are true?

A friend is someone who:

a. Sees the best in you
b. Celebrates with you when you succeed
c. Is genuinely sorry when you lose
d. Can tell you when you're wrong without totally devastating you
e. Doesn't criticize you—or laugh—when your goals keep changing
f. Supports your dreams and encourages you to take risks
g. Explains what you mean when you can't explain it yourself
h. Protects your feelings when you leave yourself vulnerable
i. Can put a positive spin on the most disastrous events to help you feel better
j. All of the above

The answer is *j*, of course—all of the above. It looks like a lot to live up to, and it is, but you're probably filling a lot of these requirements with your friends already. It takes hard work to keep friendships alive, especially at the beginning, but it's worth the effort.

Safety in Numbers

There is no better time to have a jam-packed circle of friends than when you are in your teens. You'll have more time in these years to devote yourself to nurturing friendships than you ever will again (until retirement). Responsibilities like a career and family will eat into your time. You might as well develop a good foundation of friendship now, so that you can slip into maintenance mode later. And why not introduce your friends to each other? It rarely diminishes one friendship to share it, and being able to spend time with several friends at once comes in handy as your life gets busier.

We can't say enough about expanding your options, here. Exposing yourself to the mind-sets of only a few can be dangerous to your social health. It won't take long before you exhaust all your original ideas and eventually there will be nothing new to challenge or enlighten you. "Clique people" are destined to recycle the same notions over and over again. It's like a garden pond with a broken air pump—if nothing new gets through to you are going to stagnate. We're talking mold, mildew, and odors. Is that how you want to end up?

Taking Time to Smell the Roses

Friends can have little rituals or traditions, just as families do. If you make a conscious effort to create some, you'll find you take great comfort from the activities that are special to a particular relationship. Sometimes, these evolve when you're looking the other way. For example, you go for a long walk with a particular pal, eat a pack of bubble gum apiece, blow monster bubbles, and have a great time. By the third time you've repeated this, it's become your "thing." You might even feel strange if you do it with a different friend—as if you're "cheating" on the first friend! These little rituals will bring you closer and give you a sense of exclusiveness.

At least once a year, six of my friends and I will have a sleepover at someone's house. We set an alarm to wake us up before dawn (if we aren't still up). Then we throw our coats on over our pajamas and hike down to the water to do a group salute to the sunrise.

My friend Laurie and I are huge fans of this local band in our city. We see every single performance. We used to try to scheme up ways we could get the guys in the band to notice us. My brother called us pathetic groupies and said we'd never get to meet them. But one night, we met someone who knew one of the

Ideas for Girl Get-togethers

Room Redecorating Party. Stencil a border along one wall or paint the trim a funky color. Reorganize the furniture. Get a cheap string of twinkle lights and twist them around the headboard or window.

• • •

Chefs-in-Training. Potluck suppers give you an opportunity to try out your cooking skills. Select a theme country and assign a course to each friend: soup, salad, appetizer, main course, and dessert. Or host a "Utensil Dinner," where you put together a selection of utensils (wooden spoon, garlic press, tongs, etc.) and have your friends choose which one they want to use to eat their entire meal—before they know what is being served. (Try spaghetti!)

• • •

Photo Shoot. Tell the girls to come over for a photo session and bring some interesting outfits like old bridesmaid dresses or articles of clothing they've received as gifts but would never be caught dead in.

• • •

Psychic Night. We all want to hear what life holds for us, so "rent" a psychic to come over for the evening (everyone kicks in some bucks) to give all of you a reading. Or fake it. Someone can play psychic and refer to her Magic 8 Ball or Tarot cards for spiritual guidance.

• • •

The Show Must Go On. Choose a play, movie, or musical and put on a very bad performance of it in someone's basement. Tell no one. Take photos. You will laugh your heads off every time you see them. Better yet, videotape it.

*guys in the band and we **did** get to meet them. I swear one of the greatest moments of my life was slipping that backstage pass under my brother's bedroom door.*

When you've made a real effort to do something out of the ordinary, something that's really fun, the memories you'll take away will be particularly clear and lasting.

Thank You for Being a Friend

Well, girlfriends, we want to offer you some final words of advice: Appreciate your friends and let them know it. They won't hang around if they feel you're taking them for granted. You've chosen each and every one of them carefully, so show them how much they mean to you by doing something nice. It doesn't have to be a grand gesture.

✳ Give her the royal treatment. Have her over for tea and a home-baked treat (like scones or muffins) that you baked. Use the real china.

✳ Ask to hear that story about how she met her boyfriend one more time. Really listen to her. Yes, we know you've heard it a million times—that's why it's a gesture!

✳ Make a scrapbook for her out of a blank notebook. Decorate the cover with a collage of photos of her with her friends and family.

✳ Send her a funny card or letter through the mail, "just because."

✳ If she's had a recent success, host a small celebration.

✳ Do her hair and makeup before that big date.

Many people will walk in and out of your life, but only true friends will leave footprints on your heart.
—*Eleanor Roosevelt*

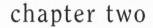

chapter two

She's My Best Friend, and I Hate Her

As the old saying goes, "Into every friendship a little rain must fall." Okay, so that's not exactly how the old saying goes, but it's true that there's a 99 percent chance of precipitation in every friendship. No matter how close you are, ladies, sooner or later, you're going to get wet. In fact, the closer you are to one special friend, the greater the likelihood of rain clouds gathering. It's pretty predictable, really. There is a direct relationship between how much time you're spending in another girl's back pocket and the severity of the storm. One day, she'll just up and do something you consider a violation and KABOOM! Often, a storm is just what's needed. It pushes out the hot, oppressive air and leaves clear skies in its wake.

You've probably heard thunder rumbling in your friendships before now. Just as hot and cold air masses spark up a storm when they rub up against each other, human beings who inhabit a confined space will inevitably create some friction as well. That space can be literal, as in the house you share with your family, or figurative, as in hanging out with your friends. We humans need breathing room or we get edgy and start looking for something to get fussed about.

You probably won't need to look very far. You're all facing so many changes right now that there's plenty to be stressed about. It's a wonder that things aren't continually stormy in your friendships, given this state of constant tension. Or maybe they are! At any rate, you will need to develop some effective strategies for dealing with conflict, which, incidentally, will give you the basics for resolving problems with everyone in your life.

Quiz

How do you rate at keeping the peace in your friendships?

Choose the answers that best suit how you'd handle each situation:

1. **Your girlfriend Grace has a new boyfriend. In your mind, he is the biggest loser in the school. Do you:**
   a. Let loose with both barrels and tell her exactly what you think of him?
   b. Become overtly rude to him whenever you are with them?
   c. Ask enough questions to make sure he's treating her well, but keep your mouth closed?
   d. Tell Grace how happy you are that she has a boyfriend and encourage her to spend as much time with him as she can? A guy is worth having at any sacrifice.

2. **Amanda is constantly whining about her family: her brother's a slob, her mom's a nag, and her dad thinks he's young and funny. So you:**
   a. Tell her she couldn't be more right—they are a bunch of losers. In fact, you trash them even when Amanda isn't complaining about them.
   b. Agree with her that they are a bit strange and say you're sure glad they aren't your family.
   c. Keep your comments to yourself. If she wants to trash her family, you'll listen, but you aren't about to start trashing them

too. You even try to point out something nice about them now and then.

d. Make yourself available to her anytime she wants to vent about them. Even if you had other plans, you break them, she needs to vent *now*. And don't burden her with any of your own family problems, because she's upset enough as it is.

3. **You have a part-time job and Cindy doesn't. You're at the mall together and she points out a dress that she absolutely LOVES but can't afford. Well, now that she's brought it to your attention, you love it too and you can afford it. What do you do?**
   a. Buy the dress right then and there. It's not your fault she doesn't have the cash.
   b. Walk away today, but head back there and buy it tomorrow. If you wait a couple of weeks to wear it, she won't even care about it anymore.
   c. You are in dire need of a dress and you really love it, but unless she genuinely encourages you to buy it, you look in other stores for something equally amazing.
   d. Use your hard-earned money to buy the dress for her. She'd look even better in it than you do!

4. **You've known Maggie since third grade. Every Saturday morning she takes swimming lessons, where she's met a girl she really likes named Ashley. One day, Maggie invites you to go swimming with the two of them. Ashley is pretty cool and you hit it off with her right away, so you:**
   a. Give Ashley a call during the week to see if she wants to go to a movie with you—her choice. You don't mention it to Maggie.
   b. Tell Maggie that you have two free passes for a movie, but since she hates horror flicks, you've asked Ashley to go with you this time.
   c. Ask Maggie if she wants to go to the movie with you. If she declines, say you don't want to go alone and ask if she thinks Ashley might go with you.
   d. Decide that Maggie seems to have much more fun with Ashley than she does with you so you give them the free movie passes.

So—how are your friend ratings? If you've chosen:

Mostly *as*: You, honey, are a friend's worst nightmare! You're worse than bad hair before a big date. Clean up your act and start being a lot more considerate or get ready for some long, lonely days ahead.

Mostly *bs*: You must find yourself wondering why your friends are annoyed with you all the time. You're acting selfishly and you'd better watch your step.

Mostly *cs*: Congratulations! You are a kind and considerate friend. You treat people with respect, and as a result you can look forward to rewarding friendships all your life.

Mostly *ds*: Do you ever get tired of people wiping their muddy boots all over you, or do you enjoy life as a doormat? Friendship has its limits, you know. People don't expect—or even want—you to sacrifice everything for them.

A Simple Rule

There is a fundamental rule of friendship that you've probably heard before: Do unto others as you would have them do unto you. No doubt you want to be treated with kindness, generosity, and respect. So you'll want to offer the same to your pals. It doesn't take much time to ask yourself, "How would I feel if she did that to me?"

It gets a bit more complicated if you ask another good question, "How would she feel if I did that to her?" It's not as if you can climb into her brain, after all, and as similar as you both may be, you won't feel the same way about every issue. What's annoying and hurtful to her might not bother you at all. Sometimes you'll be convinced a friend is deliberately trying to hurt you, but it's just that she doesn't see how what she did could ever bother you.

It's tough to focus on how others feel when you're quite naturally focused on personal development these days. Let's face it, it's tough to think about others at any time of our lives! We're born with a narcissistic streak a mile wide (How do I love me, let me count the ways . . .), but most of us rein it in as the years roll by. Right now, you and your pals are struggling with conflicting needs to fit in with your peers and yet carve out individual personalities at the same time. You may find that just as you are trying to spread your wings, you accidentally (mostly) bash the person who is always next to you. It's like taking an aerobics class when the gym is too crowded—the music is pounding, you're pumped, but you can't find an inch to move.

When you've been spending every possible moment with a close friend, you end up feeling as though you're sharing your identity with somebody else. Your friend's close proximity didn't bug you yesterday, but today for some reason you want her to get the heck out of your bubble. And she's *always* there. Suddenly everything that girl does is annoying.

Generally, two things will cause good friends to fight:

1. You're trying to shake things up and define your individuality by experimenting with some new images, styles, or philosophies, and she keeps copying you because she wants things to remain the same.
2. She is trying to be totally different by doing everything in reverse to the way you guys have always done things, and you feel left behind.

In these turbulent times, it will be difficult to maintain your expectations of each other. Because you are both changing, some of your old habits may become outdated. Often, you don't get around to re-examining them until something happens to force the situation—round about the time you're seeing the storm clouds on the horizon. The problems begin when one of you finally takes that initial step toward redefining things. For example, let's say the two of you *always* hang out together on Saturday night. Then you meet a guy and want to spend some Saturday nights with him. She doesn't acknowledge your need to change by offering to meet a different night once in a while. You finally suggest it and she looks hurt. You don't want to desert her, yet you're annoyed because she's being totally unreasonable!

When you find yourself in conflict—and it's going to happen—you need to tread very carefully. It's easy to put someone on the defensive,

Principles For Surviving Rough Weather

1. Smart Girls Say Little.

No matter how much a friend may be annoying you at the time of a fight, you will probably end up being good friends again, so avoid dissing her to your other friends during a temporary "time-out." Remember, loose lips sink friendships. Imagine how your friend will feel when she hears all the terrible things you said about her. You know you spoke in anger and didn't really mean them, but your friend won't. Although a fight won't sink your friendship, this kind of treachery just might.

2. Smart Girls Never Say It in Writing

It's probably that fear of confrontation, but girls often take it into their heads when they're annoyed to get it all down in a letter or e-mail. It's a big mistake. Why? Because you'll likely say the things you're afraid to say to her face—and there's a good reason you're afraid! Writing creates the illusion of distance and detachment. It gives you false courage because you can't see the angry or hurt expressions of your reader. Worse, it takes away her power to reply to your comments, and this can increase her anger and frustration. Another problem is that it isn't easy to convey tone effectively when you are writing about a touchy subject. You'll likely feel great as you deliver your letter. But once cooler minds prevail, don't be surprised to find yourself sneaking around trying to get it back.

And here's the worst thing. When you've long since forgotten there was ever a conflict, that letter is a lasting testament to your anger. She's got it and she probably won't throw it out. She might just wave it under your nose in a year, bringing up your words out of context. If you'd just told her face-to-face how you felt, you'd have nothing to worry about.

3. Smart Girls Never Play the Drama Queen.

Even when she's obviously in the right, a smart girl doesn't go overboard with her reactions. Someone who has been your friend for a long time generally deserves the benefit of the doubt, regardless of the circumstances. Yes, she's violated one of your friendship rules, but you should try to forgive her and get on with it. Don't drag things out and make her suffer. Your dignity and grace will earn her admiration and gratitude. Be the bigger person and put it all behind you. And that means, *put it all behind you*. Don't drag it out later and go over it again.

4. Smart Girls Never Hit Below the Belt.

The problem with fighting with a close friend is that she usually knows all your vulnerabilities. In other words, she has something on you. If you've never kissed a guy and you're sensitive about it, she could bring it up in a fight. Of course, you'll have stuff on her, too. Maybe she thinks she's not very bright. Are you going to use that? Never! Friendships are based on trust, and you need to play fair. Keep it clean, ladies. No mud wrestling. Stick to the subject at hand and don't let it get too personal. The below-the-belt comments are the ones that neither of you will ever forget.

5. Smart Girls Imitate Boys.

Guys have the edge on us in this respect—they fight clean. When chicks fight, they often use sneaky girl tactics. They say personal, hurtful things. They use clever, slippery words. They overanalyze. They drag it out. They sulk. How do we know? Because we've done it.

We've also watched a lot of guys fight over the years, and here's what happens: They get into huge blowouts where there is shouting and name-calling and maybe some pushing. It's ugly—and then it's over. They shut it down and shoot hoops together. An hour later, they're slapping each other on the back and laughing. They just get over it.

Skip the analysis and put it behind you. It's more important to patch things up than to figure out exactly where the blame rests. Reach out with a gesture. No, don't snap a wet towel on her butt in the change room as the guys do, but find something that your friend will recognize as a white flag and start waving.

and then you've already lost the fight, even though you might have a very valid point. Your best bet is to communicate how you feel without accusing her of deliberately trying to hurt you. For example, you can say, "I know you don't mean to, Cecilia, but I can't help feeling hurt when you say you'll call and you don't." You want her to understand why you are upset, and work things out. It's better not to attack her, causing her mind to snap shut so she can't listen. Imagine her reaction if you say, "I really hate it when you get so caught up with *Cameron* (snide tone) that you don't call me when you say you will." Tone counts! If she hears "snide" in it, it doesn't much matter what words you're using, you'll be struck by lightning.

Girls of all ages tend to dislike confrontation, so you may not get to air your views if you don't go about it the right way. You may barely work your eyebrows into a frown before you hear the door slamming and footsteps running off into the distance. She's gone and you're left with unfinished business. It doesn't mean you shouldn't share your concerns just because you think she won't like them. If you feel you've been mistreated, you owe it to yourself and to her to do all you can to save the friendship.

We can't look into our crystal ball and see what's in another person's heart, so sometimes we have to ask. Try the following:

1. Wait until you feel you can share your concerns in a calm, reasonable way.
2. Pick a moment when you are alone and you are both relaxed (i.e., not when you're both studying for a big exam).
3. Ease into the conversation by asking how she's been or what's been on her mind. Maybe she's been upset about something else. If she has, empathize by trying to understand what she's been going through.
4. Explain—without heat (or ice!) in your voice—that you've been a bit upset lately about something she did or said.
5. If she looks genuinely surprised, tell her you know she didn't deliberately hurt your feelings.
6. Let her explain, without rushing or interrupting her, how she feels about the situation.

7. Listen for regret in her voice, and respect in her words. Be willing to accept that. It's usually enough.
8. If you don't hear regret and respect, ask if she understands why you are upset. Sometimes she won't, and you'll have to explain it differently.
9. If you have differing views of the situation, you're looking at that frustrating word *compromise*. You may need to agree to disagree, or to do things her way one week, your way another. Compromise is good. You must give to receive, but pride and respect remain intact.

Although many things can lead to disagreement and dispute in a friendship, they rarely destroy it. Usually, a temporary break will help. It will allow you both to cool off and put things in perspective. Besides, there's nothing like spending time with a new bunch of people you don't like nearly as well to help you appreciate your friend's many virtues.

Curtain Calls

Unfortunately, some friendships come to an end. This is always sad, no matter what caused the break. Sometimes, it's as simple as nothing. You have nothing in common anymore, so you just spend less and less time together. Maybe your friend is trying to change so much about her life that she decides to clean house completely, and you find yourself "shelved" simply because you don't suit her new lifestyle. Don't sweat it too much. You need to put your energies into friends who appreciate who you are. But we know it hurts just the same.

On the other hand, you can have long diversions on the highway of life and link up with pals again later on. People suit you better at different times. It's a long, winding road and you may be surprised where it takes you.

Even friendships that end can bring surprising gifts. A friend can enter your life, brighten it for a time, then disappear. But the glow can last long after the person is gone, because you still have the memories of the good times you had, and the knowledge of how the friendship changed you.

Zara was too cool to be friends with Alison in high school. She had tons of boyfriends and tons of confidence and Alison was terribly shy. In their first year of university, however, they found themselves in the same class among hundreds of strangers. Zara pushed Alison to do what she really wanted to do, which was sing. She was so impressed by Alison's talent that she sought out the manager of the student club and asked him to let Alison perform. Zara came to every performance for a year, but then she moved away and eventually, the two lost touch. Alison is still sad about this, but each time she thinks of Zara, she remembers the confidence she gained through Zara's support. In fact, she believes that Zara's belief in her gave her courage to start a career as a singer.

Last Rites

How will you know when enough is enough? Basically, it's when the friendship never makes you feel good about yourself. Anytime someone else's influence brings you down or forces you to behave like someone you're not, it's a sneaky little hurricane just waiting to blow up into gale-force winds. You'll hear a faint howling in the eaves and wonder, "Why do I feel pressured whenever she's around?" Your parents will start saying she's a bad influence. Then your other friends will start dropping like flies, because they don't like her. And suddenly, one day, you'll realize you don't like yourself when you're with her.

There's a difference between cutting some slack for a friend who is going through a phase and letting her take advantage of you. If a friendship makes you feel bad about yourself for too long, it's time to cut your losses. Friendships are supposed to be fun and constructive. Don't put up with one that's destructive. By this we mean a friendship that destroys your confidence because someone runs you down or neglects you. Maybe she spreads rumors about you at school, yet pretends to be your pal. Maybe she says horrible things about other people and shows that her values are different from yours. Or maybe she commits a more obvious crime, like stealing your boyfriend or telling your family secrets. Whatever it is, do yourself a favor and move on. You give the best and you deserve it in return. That's it—no compromising on this one.

Success Enough for All

Most of the time, you'll be able to weather the storms that pass through your friendships quite nicely. It's important to keep in mind that they change just as everything else changes in life, and change can be uncomfortable. It's scary. When a friendship starts evolving, usually one person initiates it. The other person may feel threatened: "What if there's no room for me in her exciting new life?"

This insecurity can open the door to competitive feelings. You may feel the need to branch out and develop some new interests; when you do, your friend worries that you're breaking away from her. So she may try to tag along. Remember that you can't lay claim to these interests. It doesn't mean your competitive friend will get exactly the same thing out of it and it shouldn't affect your enjoyment.

And don't let your own competitive feelings slow you down. Just because your pal succeeds at something doesn't mean there isn't plenty of success left over for you. There are enough good marks, cute guys, and awards to go around. Too often we feel that someone's success decreases our chance at it. It doesn't. In fact, success is contagious. If she's breaking ground, follow in her footsteps for a few steps, then branch out on your own. We don't all want the same things. Why are you following her around on a horse when she's a natural and you'd rather be running track? It's easier to compete in a completely different arena and take home your own rewards. Then you can keep on believing in each other's phenomenal talents without getting distracted by the small stuff.

One word of caution: Hold her back at your peril. If you have a friendship with heart, it can take a lot of stretching. Sometimes you just have to trust that people will wander off and snap back. Even if she doesn't, it's still better to have let go. There's no happiness in a friendship that's forced.

When all else fails, it helps to believe that things happen for a reason. The design may not be apparent right away, but if you look back in a few years, you'll see why things happened the way they did. If one girl hadn't moved on, perhaps you wouldn't have met your new friend—and isn't she the one who convinced you to try jazz dancing, which it turns out is one of your hidden talents? There's an activity out there that has your name written all over it, and chances are it will be a friend who guides you to it.

chapter three

My Girlfriend Has a New Boyfriend, and I Don't

*I*t's always a horrible day when you realize that your mother is right about something, isn't it? But isn't she the one who told you first that life isn't fair? We wish we could say it ain't so, but you'll bump your head against this truth all your life. Sometimes, despite the fact that you are just as clever and just as good as someone else, she will get something that you don't. No matter how hard you wish and work, Fate may see fit to send the reward to your friend instead. No, life isn't fair at all.

One minute you and your best buddy are having a blast spending Saturday nights looking for love in all the right places and the next, she finds it. Now you're home alone, looking for love and friendship on TV. The way it was supposed to work, dammit, is that you were going to find love *together*, with two studly guys who are also best friends, so that you could become a fabulous foursome. Fate clearly mixed up your order.

Or maybe Fate does grant you this happiness, just not for very long. Say you meet and date two guys who are best pals and harmony prevails. Well, at least until the day things take a nasty turn for you and Lover Boy, and it's Splitsville, U.S.A. Meanwhile, your friend is still head over heels for her guy and he is still tight with your ex. Can you say awkward? You've become a third wheel faster than you can hum "Show Me the Meaning of Being Lonely," and you're back to spending Saturday night on the couch again. Or worse, you get your friend's company on weekends only by default when her beau has a hockey practice. Then you have to listen to her blather on endlessly about Slapshot Boy, as if he's the next Great One. You didn't mind this at all a few weeks ago when life with your own beau, Mr. High Sticking, was oh-so-fine, but now that you're in the penalty box, you wish she'd just shut up.

Woe is You

"Hell hath no fury like a woman scorned," Shakespeare said, and he's so right. Whether it's a guy or a girlfriend who's doing the scorning, that "dumped" feeling sure throws your world off-kilter. You lie there in the Dumpster, looking up at the sky and wondering how it happened that you were tossed out like yesterday's crusty Kraft Dinner.

When it's your best friend giving you the boot for a guy, you'll find a new and toxic emotion pouring into you. It's jealousy, babies—the green-eyed monster. You'll experience bitter envy many times in life, but rarely will it be keener than over adolescent love. It's totally natural and it's totally honest, but pretty? Uh-uh.

So what will you be pondering, there in the Dumpster? Well, you'll be very busy rationalizing. That means you'll be scheming up explanations for how you feel that are probably not terribly honest. This is something we all do because it's difficult to confront the ugliness of jealousy in ourselves. Better to call it something else, like righteous anger: "How dare she throw me away like stale day-olds after all I've done for her?" Or devastating hurt: "I cry every time I think about how close we used to be, before she wrecked everything." Or stunned bewilderment: "I just can't understand how she could treat me like this." Your rationalizing will keep you busy for a while, but you are still lying on a pile of moldy garbage and it stinks in there. So get up, give yourself a good shake, and clamber out of your despair.

Sure, she's treated you badly, but you loved her last month for her many virtues and they didn't disappear overnight. They've just been temporarily obscured by her frenzy of luv. If you've already experienced the scourge of hormones, you shouldn't be too surprised. Mind you, once they settle down again, it's hard to remember and acknowledge just how much power hormones have to disorient.

It's not like anyone sets out to change when she meets a guy. She just wants to move in a bit closer to her Love Bunny and bask in his glow. But that glow often ignites a fire, and with the resulting heat and smoke, it's easy for her to forget she has a life outside that is cool and comfortable. Friends? What friends? She might vaguely recall some girls she used to hang around with. They meant something to her once, but that was before she realized how cozy it is in the inferno.

Hormones. They're trouble. In girls and guys of all ages, they overcome reason and urge people to do all kinds of things they wouldn't do ordinarily. This time, the victim is your best friend. Next time, you could be the one who gets sucked into the furnace.

The Other Side of the Story

We know you don't begrudge your friend her romance. It's just that you want to have one, too. And if Fate is only doling out one favor right now, shouldn't that romance go to you? You *need* it more. It would really help you to be a better, happier person. If you were blessed with a Love Bunny all your own, you wouldn't forget your friend and throw yourself into the romance to the exclusion of all else, would you? You'd never desert her and make her feel like rubbish, right?

Wrong. You'll succumb to the madness in about two seconds and start thinking about your new romance morning, noon, and night. If you get a second's reprieve from your obsessing, sure you'll give her a call (mostly to tell her how great he is). But you'll already be out of touch. You can lose that valuable connection very quickly. Friendships between girls are often based on knowing everything about each other's lives. You can't get to that place of familiarity—or stay there—if you don't do the time.

You think that you can catch up with your friend in a few months when the mania ends. Wrong again, honey. Your wonderful friendship may never be the same. A little bit of the trust will be gone, because she'll know that you could disappear at any moment and leave her stranded. Meanwhile, you'll grow stale on your new love—or worse, he could put you out to pasture.

The Whys and Wherefores

Why do we dump our friends? We know, deep down in our hearts, that this is not Mr. Right—just Mr. Right *Now*. After all, how many people marry their first loves, their high school sweethearts? Not many. And if they do, they often regret it. So for this you dump your girlfriends? Not a wise decision. You firmly believe that your friends will understand and that they'll forgive all. They might, but why take the chance? Don't they deserve a little more respect?

If you have one best friend and she "acts up" when you link up with a guy, you might be tempted to dismiss her distress as jealousy. Yes, she probably is jealous, because she wishes she had a boy in her life too. But that doesn't mean she wishes that you *didn't* have one. There's a big difference. What your friend really wants is (1) for both of you to have boyfriends, so that you can bond over analyzing their every move; or (2) for you to spend a respectable amount of time with her, including some weekend nights, so that you can support her in finding a love of her own; or (3) if all else fails for you to be single again *by choice*. She doesn't want you to be heartbroken and miserable. What good would you be to her then?

Of course, if you take our advice about having lots of good friends, you won't get into this bind. It's a problem that tends to crop up if you've limited yourself to one "best friend." If you focus all your energies on one person, the relationship is always more intense. It will be a huge shock for either of you if a guy comes on the scene and suddenly "makes three." She's your alter ego, after all, your reflection. You're delighted if something great happens to her, as long as something equally great happens to you. The Law of Best Friends means that you should always receive blessings of equal value. If only we could get Fate to obey this law!

With an intense "best" friendship, there's always a struggle for balance. Most people need to feel that it's working out to a 50:50 ratio: half the time, you do the sacrificing; the other half, she does. Sometimes it will be 80:20 for a while, but that's okay as long as it shifts back eventually and balances out. The problem with having only one friend is that it's too easy to keep score. If you spread yourself around with many friends, you'll be too busy to compare what you're giving to what you're receiving. Furthermore, when you're surrounded by great pals, it won't come as such a shock when someone pairs off and disappears for a time. But if your one and only best pal has given you the hormonal heave-ho—hello, loneliness.

Rising Above It

Whether you've been dumped by a best friend or a boyfriend, you're going to need to turn your attitude around pretty quickly. Believe us, we know how tempting it is just to plug your nose and lie there in the Dumpster feeling sorry for yourself. We've sucked in the pungent aromas of garbage in our day, too. The thing is, if you hang around the junk heap, the stink kind of sticks and, not too surprisingly, your overall appeal plummets.

Bitterness, anger, jealousy, self-pity just don't attract people. Yes, it's tough to overcome these feelings when you've been left behind, but you can't roll around in them too long. It won't help to change your situation. And ultimately, it will make things worse. If you wallow in ugly feelings, people will see the damage a mile off and run for their lives. That means boys as well as girls. You will have difficulty making new connections in your love life, and you will risk losing your other girlfriends because they will find you rotten to be around. As we said, they need to get something out of your friendship too. If you are never any fun anymore, they'll slowly disappear, like stars fading one by one from the sky.

So unless you want to live your life with no girlfriends and no romance, you might want to SNAP OUT OF IT! *Everybody* gets hurt in friendship or love at some point. If someone tells you it's never happened to her, she's either lying or you've been talking to a six-year-old.

Your Escape Route

Since we're on the pleasant subject of rejection, ladies, let's say that you simply cannot afford to lose those girlfriends. You're going to need their help to climb out of that Dumpster when a romantic disaster lands you there. This day will come, sooner or later. All those who venture into romantic relationships eventually get burned at least once, and most people *cause* a few singes too. That's just the way it goes. You'll never get anywhere in life if you just give up and mope when something doesn't work out. By all means, take a moment or two to catch your breath and collect yourself. But then, as the cliché goes, get back on that horse. If you want something, you've got to keep going after it. Eventually, you'll get what you want, or you'll discover that what you wanted wasn't the best thing for you, and you'll end up with something far better. In the meantime, celebrate your girlfriends and treat them like the queens they are.

Makin' a List, Checkin' It Twice

When you've got the girls rallied around, you will need to do some work to reconnect with them. Here are some entertaining exercises that will help you do this and will also shove you in the direction of romantic recovery.

First, make a list of all the reasons it's great to be single. This list will have you feeling better about your new single status in no time. Keep it tucked away somewhere and haul it out for a quick jolt of reality the next time you find yourself getting too carried away over some guy.

You're Single, So . . .

1. Stop pretending to be in a good mood all the time
2. Stop trying to look desirable every second of the day
3. Order your own, extra-large portion of fries—and some onion rings (No more faking that you're not hungry.)
4. Stop pretending to like his loud, obnoxious music, friends, or parents
5. Chat on the phone to friends who don't ask you to hang on while they check out what's on TV
6. Stop leaving weekend nights open until Friday when he still hasn't booked you

Another excellent way to reconnect with your gal pals and get over the failed romance is to create a list of all the synonyms you can think of for the word *penis*. We've done this in restaurants on more than one occasion, and inevitably the female staff and women from other tables join in. There's something quite magical about the power of this game to put the guy-thing in perspective. We challenge you to come up with 30 of these terms. We know there are more because we've hit at least 40, but we've been around longer to hear them. Here are a few to get you started: willy, peter, pistol, torpedo of love.

After this, move on to discussing the girliest topics you can think of: makeup, hair, lingerie, astrology, decorating, pantyhose, periods, hair, pets, childbirth, quilts, jewelry, other people, chocolate, celebrities, amazing coincidences, love stories, breakup stories, chick movies, clothes, bad dreams, fated love, perfume, weight, and so on.

Make sure you really revel in the estrogen, here. It must be the kind of conversation that would send a guy screaming from the room.

Any Excuse for a Party

Let's assume that you're starting to feel better about not having a boyfriend. In fact, you hardly ever give old what's-his-name a second thought these days. You're almost ready to start casting your line for new fish in the sea. Then, along comes some anniversary that you shared with him or—heaven forbid—Valentine's Day. The dying embers of your love burst into flames again, and you're at risk for a full-fledged relapse into self-pity. Don't panic! No need to sit home weeping silently while holding his photo.

We have the perfect solution to get rid of those lingering feelings for that boy and bond big-time with your gang of friends. Why not host a "recovery bash"? Call up all your single friends and invite them over. Tell each one to bring along some photos of the guy she can't quite get over. Even yearbook headshots will work. In fact, tell them to go to a photo-copy shop, pump up the size, and run off several color copies in different sizes. They should also bring a cheap scrapbook or a notebook and any magazines they have lying around the house. Do not go into details. There are not enough surprises like this in this world!

Recovery Bash Itinerary

To kick off the recovery bash, nothing beats a good game of darts. Not just any game of darts, mind you. This one has a special set of rules. First, you need to locate a dartboard and a set of darts (obviously). Someone you know is bound to have them. Then round up all your markers and other art supplies. Have everybody swap their photos and get busy embellishing them with bad mustaches, devil's horns, blacked-out teeth—you know the routine. Pin the photo of a heartbreaker on the dartboard. The girl who got spurned does the honors by throwing the first round of darts. Once she's hit it, it's open season for the rest of you. Take turns throwing darts at that photo until Mr. Wrong is full of holes. Then move on to the next photo. The game is over when the images on the photographs are no longer recognizable. And the best part is, everybody wins!

When you're ready for your next activity, grab the stack of magazines. Cut out some photos of voluptuous, scantily clad girls (easy to find in any mag!)—minus their beautiful heads. Glue the bodies into your scrapbooks. Now, take your photos of Mr. Heartbreak and glue his head on top of these lovely gals. There's nothing quite as satisfying—and poisonous to a long-held crush—as seeing Boy Wonder's head on a girlie bod.

If you're Suzy Homemaker types, another enjoyable activity is making the Quilt of Exs. Oh, nothing fancy, don't you worry. Take any old piece of fabric (a square foot will do) and create an artistic rendering of your former beau and any meaningful symbols of your time together. The goal is to hang it up, so keep it tame, ladies. Use sparkles and sequins and any groovy art supplies you have lying around. If someone is good with a needle, she can run these together on a sewing machine or perhaps one of the mothers will participate. Then you all can take turns displaying this fine piece of commemorative artwork in your bedrooms. As the host of this recovery bash, you will be the first keeper of the quilt and you will pass it to the next victim of heartbreak at the appropriate time. Each time there is a new breakup, a new square should be created.

For those with a flair for the dramatic, try inventing movie plots with all the guys who have let you down as the main characters. Make their characters as undesirable as possible. Don't hold back. They should be painfully uncool, gross, boring, extremely nerdy, wart covered, and freaky to the max. Then give them some interesting quirks, like a taste for chocolate milk with salsa. Let your imaginations run wild. Next, choose a scenario: a murder mystery, a Wild West adventure, or a mob movie. It doesn't really matter, just make sure that their characters endure hard times and that the movie ends in absolute disaster. You'll laugh, you'll cry, you'll love it. Write your screenplays down in your Recovery Scrapbooks for posterity.

You could also dig out your old Barbie and Ken dolls (we know you still have them) and act out scenes in which *you* come off looking fabulous. Barbie can say all the clever lines you wish you'd said to him. This is constructive, because you are rehearsing for the next time you're in a similar situation.

Some tunes would really liven up your evening, too, so how about taking some lyrics from favorite songs and changing them to defame your lost prince? Better yet, if you can stand it, desecrate "your song," the one you shared with him. Sing your new songs out loud before gluing the new lyrics into your Recovery Scrapbook.

Whatever you do, be as funny as you can, because humor will help you regain your perspective on your dear departed beau, and humor will bind you to your gal pals. Remember how we talked about making memories, earlier on? It's the emotion surrounding an event that engraves it in your memory. Laughter brings happiness, and what started out as a negative situation will spin around 180 degrees to be very positive. Can you imagine the pleasure those scrapbooks will bring you in the future when you're feeling a little down about anything at all? Rough day at school? Flip open your book and remember an evening of hysterical laughter. Perspective in seconds.

Before this party is over, you must all take a vow of silence. Keep your scrapbooks under lock and key if you can. Your Recovery Rituals must never be revealed to outsiders (e.g., boys).

Your top-secret rituals, whatever they are, will have great power. You'll know that at the end of any romantic relationship, there will be one heck of a party. The fun, the food, the bad behavior will remind you that that you have a solid foundation of friendships with women, no matter what happens in the treacherous world of love.

To our minds, there can't be enough celebrations of girls' friendships. Chick bonding in any shape or form is life affirming. The traditions you establish now can be carried on for decades, and modified to
suit your changing circumstances. We just heard about one woman in
her forties who gathered her friends for a divorce party. She spray-
painted her wedding veil black and wore it throughout the feast. Of
course, there was plenty of liquor at that party. As your scrapbooks and
catalogues grow fatter, you'll get to the legal age where you can toast to
the passing of your Heartbreakers with real champagne if you like. In
the meantime, make it soda, but do make the toast. "Goodbye to Jack,
who broke my heart and hello again to my pals, who see me through
tough times. May we spend many more happy hours together."

Single and Loving It

Yes, there is life after boys. You'll have some great times once you've said
good-bye to him. With your girlfriends, you can totally be yourself
because you know they accept you just the way you are. So celebrate
your friends and revel in your single status. There is much to enjoy
without a boyfriend. In fact, although it may be nice to have one occasionally, it can be a hell of a lot more fun just to *look* for one. The thrill
of the chase is usually better than the catch anyway.

part two

They're Goofy,
They're Gross,
and Damn It,
They're Great!

Let's Talk About Boys

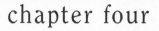

chapter four

Through His Eyes

*H*ave you ever sat through a movie with a guy only to find out later that he apparently watched a totally different film? You saw a love story where the devotion of the leading characters overcame terrible hardship. He saw an adventure flick where the hero stopped conquering natural disasters only long enough to have sex with some fabulous babe. You emerge from the theater drained, with your mascara running. He's charged up. "That was so sad," you say. "Sad?" he asks, looking puzzled. "It was *hilarious*. Did you see the way he sawed off the dinosaur's wing?" How could he have missed the whole point of that movie?

Welcome to the real world of boys and girls, where even a minor exchange of information can be a complex and baffling exercise in misunderstanding. We are worlds apart physically and emotionally, and our points of view often collide quite forcefully. We're going to give you as many tips and observations about boys as we can in these chapters, but we don't have all the answers. It's impossible for a girl to crawl inside a boy's mind, because there is a fundamental biological difference that prevents complete understanding. You can blame almost everything on the fact that they have one chromosome—the Y chromosome—that we don't have. A chromosome is a tiny piece of genetic material that the eye cannot see, but it packs a mighty big punch. It's the one that makes them taller, hairier, and more muscular than we are, and it's the cause of their abundance of testosterone. It's amazing how this one thing can make their life experience so different from ours.

One-Track Minds

We know that making sweeping generalizations about a whole group of people is a very bad habit, but we won't let that slow us down here. So, let's have some fun. We'll begin by giving you a preliminary look into the boy brain.

One of your biggest sources of frustration with males throughout your life will be that they don't like sharing their feelings. But there's a very good reason the guy who fascinates you most is not sharing what's going on in his head. He learned early, likely at his mother's knee, that his thoughts are better kept to himself when women are around—unless he's trying to bug them.

In every boy's mind, there's an interior monologue in progress that is constantly being screened for offensive content, which, when detected, is simultaneously translated into something that is safe for girls' ears. Bear in mind that with a teenager, the screening device may be on overload by 10 A.M. Here are a few examples of how simultaneous translation works:

> *He says:* "You look great in those pants."
> *He's thinking: "Your butt looks great in those pants."*
> *He says (over the phone):* "What are you wearing?"
> *He's thinking: "Please tell me you're walking around completely nude."*
> *He says:* "Of course, I'm glad to be here with you instead of playing ball with the guys."
> *He's thinking: "I hope we get to make out before your parents get home."*
> *He says:* "I didn't even notice her. I was looking at the Porsche."
> *He's thinking: "There is not enough Spandex in the world."*

You get the picture. It's often a little shocking for girls to realize just how much guys think about sex. In fact, it interferes with their reception of any other information. They do learn early that girls don't think about sex in quite the same way, however, and this can generate a lot of guilt about their natural urges. You'll often see hints of this frustration in their behavior. Don't take advantage of it, though. The way we're wired is out of our hands. All we can do is have patience with each other and learn how to live with our legacy.

It's Prehistoric

Some experts say that human beings came from the sea and evolved into the fine species we've become. In fact, they say human evolution likely stopped several hundred thousand years ago when we'd developed sufficiently to conquer our world. Now, if we did stop evolving that long ago, is it any wonder that our meeting and mating behaviors are confusing in the modern world?

Primitive men and women were hunters and gatherers. They scrounged out a meager living hunting animals and picking roots and berries. With basic survival at stake every day, there wasn't a lot of time for the niceties of courtship. Your female ancestors likely contemplated whether a cave boy would make a good provider for her and the future kids, while he checked her out to see if she looked like a good, healthy breeder.

Romantic? No. Natural? Afraid so. Today, males and females alike have many urges that are suited to a very different time. Some of them don't make much sense in a modern setting, but it's important to remember that our meeting and mating strategies have served us surprisingly well—to the tune of over 7 billion people on the planet. The numbers speak for themselves.

Today it isn't acceptable for Mr. Neanderthal to grab you as you're picking berries and drag you off to show you the etchings in his cave. What you need to consider, however, is that on an instinctual level, he might find that far easier than the modern approach. The old ways were direct. As this new millennium begins, guys want to be nice, decent, and civilized—and they mostly are—but they have inherited a few habits from earlier times, just as we have.

All this means is that there's a lot of room for confusion between males and females at any time, especially in adolescence. You'll think guys are completely weird, and believe us, they're no better at figuring you out. That's the great equalizer, you see. Most teenage boys haven't the foggiest notion about how to handle a girl.

The many differences between the sexes will emerge over the next several chapters, but we'll start with four simple comparisons to get you started.

Paralysis by Analysis. You like to analyze social situations with your friends. You find it interesting and enjoyable to sit for hours discussing all the intricate details of human relationships.

He likes to analyze the weekend's sports scores, motors, and the tangled innards of lab rats in biology class. He's a doer. Contemplating emotion paralyzes him.

My Eyes Adored You. You have eyes only for your true love of the moment. You like to feel special in your relationship, knowing that he only has eyes for you. He has eyes for you, and for just about every other girl. He can't help it, but the nice ones develop a skill for scanning without moving their heads.

Allow Me. You're capable of figuring out how to hook up the family's new VCR on your own. You can read, so you peruse the manual. He wants to perform a service for you. The more brute strength or technical genius it requires, the better. You'd love to have him send a romantic card, but to him, fixing your computer is a loving gesture. All the better if you stand by for an hour and watch as he tries this without the aid of a manual.

He Says So in Subtle Ways–Not! You beat around the bush and leave subtle hints like a trail of breadcrumbs when you want something. It works beautifully with your girlfriends. He says what he means or he says nothing at all. There's no subtlety there. He won't focus on what you're saying long enough to ferret out hidden meanings in your words. To get his attention, you must be brief and to the point.

One of the Guys

In the realm of boy-girl relationships, there exists an interesting middle ground. It's a sort of crossover zone where you are able to infiltrate the enemy camp. For just a short time, you may be invited to become "one of the boys." Although the venture is not without risk, it does provide a valuable opportunity to gain information.

There's something we need to tell you before you go over the lines, however: Men are animals. Tell you something you *don't* know? Okay, then: So are you. Somehow we humans think we are separate from (and above) the rest of the animal kingdom, but the truth is, we are very much a part of it. We are primates, just like gorillas and chimpanzees. In fact, we share 98 percent of the exact same DNA (the basic building block of life) with chimps. Imagine, if you will, a chimp in a nice pair of jeans and a sweatshirt. Isn't he looking just the faintest bit like your latest crush? No? How about after he breaks your heart? Now you're seeing the resemblance!

Well, take a look in the mirror and ponder that 98 percent. If it's not on our faces, it's gotta be hiding somewhere. Sure, chimps have a whole lot more body hair, but chances are we are going to share other similarities—possibly even our approaches to mating. It's shocking, yes, but if you accept that we're all animals, it will make your trip into the Boy Zone far easier.

Let us tell you about the cute little desert rat that lives in the land of the cactus. The female stakes out a territory and stays there. The male, on the other hand, is driven by a desperate need to spread his seed as widely as possible and pass on his gerbil genes to the next generation. So the male runs his little legs off visiting female after female, trying to beat out all the other males. Sadly, he dies very young. The female stays put, raises her young, and lives a good long life.

The moral of the story is: Throughout the animal kingdom, males compete and females choose. And that goes for human animals too. She who is able to bear young gets to choose. That means you, girls. We're part of this animal kingdom, where girls set the limits and guys compete for their attentions. This will be hard to believe, given some of the torments you endure in trying to interact with guys, but if you remember it, it will help you decipher much of their odd behavior and also determine where to focus your energies. It's the Desert Rat Theory of Human Sexuality.

Behind Enemy Lines

We've been there. Both of us have had plenty of opportunities to go over to the other side and hang out with the boys. It's a woman's responsibility to share the fruits of her research, so we'll describe some of the horrors we've encountered. One of us had an opportunity to work in a gym's office, which was connected to the men's locker room by a split door. Here are some startling observations made while the door was half open:

* Guys do not wear towels on the way to the shower. They strut proudly, towel thrown nonchalantly over one shoulder, manly assets swinging freely. This is done seemingly for the sake of easy comparison to other guys' assets.
* Guys do not care if women see them swinging freely on the way to the shower.
* Guys are uncomfortable when they learn that men with a different sexual preference are assessing the assets on display.
* Guys rank women, constantly assessing who's "in their league."
* Guys love sports because competing is not only condoned, it's required.
* Guys want the girl all the other guys want. It doesn't matter if she's not their type. It's the pleasure of defeating their pals that counts. Take note: Having five guys compete for your attention is not a sign that you are wearing the right cologne. It's all about them. You are the flavor of the month.

To our minds, every girl should have the chance to be the only girl in an all-guy gang. It's the ideal time to view the other team just living their lives. You'll need an invitation to go on this mission. Generally, you'll end up in their camp because a guy pal suggested you join him on an outing with his friends. Your first inclination will be to find reinforcements—in other words, another girl to go with you—but don't. That will ruin the whole dynamic. Alone, you can be "one of the guys," but two girls will be treated as outsiders. The guy who invited you will introduce you to his circle of friends with his automatic "she's okay" stamp of approval. For a time, they will forget you are a girl—as long as you don't remind them with inappropriate giggling, squealing, or gasps of horror.

Make sure you don't slip up and give away any secrets from your own camp, sister. Part of what makes girls so attractive to boys is the mystery that surrounds them. It's a major part of your appeal. When it goes, some of the fun drains out of the whole boy-girl thing for them, so put a lid on it, honey. Take all you can and leave nothing behind.

Subject: The Boys Club
Date: November 15th
From: MegAbabe<megababe@me.com>
To: TaraBull<tarabull@you.com>
Hey Tara!
I've hardly seen you lately. You've been hanging around with Josh and his friends all the time. What gives? Have you got it for Josh or am I missing something?
Later,
Meg

Subject: Got It Bad
Date: November 18th
From: TaraBull<tarabull@you.com>
To: MegAbabe<megababe@me.com>
Hi Meg,
Don't worry, I'm back where I belong. My time in the Boys' Club was a complete disaster. Yes, I was interested in Josh, and I thought he was interested too because he kept inviting me along all the time. Then he starts asking me all about Terri and whether or not she has a boyfriend. He actually said the words, "she's tasty." Oh my god! He was just being my friend to get the scoop on Terri. I've been used!
Tara

One day you'll realize with a jolt—like when an elevator drops a foot or two—that you've lost your feminine status by hanging around with the guys for too long. That's why we advise taking only short trips over the line to see how the other half lives. You're not going to want to move in!

After all, it's a waste of time to try to turn a guy into a gal pal. You won't get what you want—which is a heart-to-heart—and he will be frustrated because you're asking for something he can't give. Even if you explain specifically what you want or need, he probably won't be able to provide it. What's more, he'll feel he's letting you down and may even decide you're "high maintenance," which is not something guys put up with in pals.

There are plenty of positive things you'll discover as one of the guys. They'll take you along on a very different evening, where the conversation revolves around a particular activity, instead of the activity revolving around conversation, as it does with girls. It can be a great relief to leave all the girly analysis behind and have some uncomplicated fun. Last, but not least, it can be a real break to hang with guys who have no "love-goddess" expectations of you.

They're Nasty

One thing you can always count on when you view the teenage male in his natural habitat is plenty of bad behavior. At 15, he's barely domesticated. And the sad fact is, nothing gives a teenage boy quite so much pleasure as being able to gross you out.

> *Rachel and her friends were driving home from the amusement park one day when they saw a very cute guy at the bus stop. The light turned red just at that moment, so as they waited, Rachel waved at him. He waved back and gave her a big grin. Then, just as they started to move forward, he spun around, pulled down his pants and mooned her!*

Who among you has not been knocked over backward when a boy takes off his running shoes after a long day? And how about that crotch scratcher? In the name of research, we asked "why?" They've told us they're not even aware they're doing it. The evidence supports their story. After all, little boys, barely out of diapers, are often seen gripping their wee manhood in a public place. Perhaps guys worry their "little buddy" might just wander off one day and disappear forever. And we won't even get started on the subject of bodily functions!

Hi Tara,

I thought I'd drop you a quick note to share something about that goofball I call my boyfriend. He tells me this morning that he's written me a poem that he'll give me after school. So all day I'm totally excited and do you know what that pig-boy did? He wrote me a poem about his scabs. That's right, the scabs he got during football practice. What a knob! Or maybe I'm the idiot for expecting a sonnet! I can't believe I still want to go out with him, but I do. It was actually pretty funny but I pretended to be completely grossed out, of course. Guys!!!
Meg

Spitballs and Snowballs

Guys have dozens of confusing, and annoying, ways to express their interest in you. We can confirm your worst suspicions that a guy who taunts you is generally quite fond of you. It's hard to accept that the boy who treats you the worst is also the one who likes you the best. It makes more sense when you remember that even at the best of times, boys have a hard time expressing their emotions—let alone, sentiment. Why say it with a single rose when they can say it instead with some armpit farts in class? It does get your attention, no? And perversely, the negative attention you then provide, in the form of rolled eyes and disgusted comments ("You are such a pig, Jon.") is in some ways easier for them to deal with. Rare indeed is the 15-year-old boy who can just walk up to a girl and say, "I really like you."

Most of the time, it is easy enough to endure this bizarre behavior. It's not that much of a stretch to believe that the guy washing your face with snow is actually courting you. Your brutish admirer may also tease you about everything you hold dear. For example, he'll have no problem telling you that your favorite band sucks, even though he recently paid to attend their concert. He'll mock the jeans you wear and the books you read. He'll imitate your walk, which cannot possibly resemble that prance he performs in the school hallway. And he'll take joy from twisting everything you say into something perverted. The minute you laugh, he'll know he's winning you over and will redouble his efforts.

A Little Line Dancing

Excuse me, can I have a quarter? My mother told me to call her
    when I found my angel.
Did it hurt when you fell from heaven?
Aren't you tired? You've been running though my mind all day.
Your father must have been a thief. He stole the stars from the skies
    and put them in your eyes.
Do you believe in love at first sight, or should I walk by again?

Most guys will quit this behavior long before they hurt your feel-ings, but some are truly mean-spirited. One of these days, you'll encounter a real bully who continually criticizes everything you do, say, and wear. He'll try to make you seem stupid by ridiculing your every thought in front of others.

It's pretty hard to believe that a guy who treats you this badly is actually interested in you, but again, it's true. He just doesn't know how to handle himself. If he pays this much attention to you he's *got it bad*. What's more, he is convinced (and rightly so) that you are way out of his league. The crueler he is, the more bitter he is about his prospects of getting anywhere with you. Intentionally or not, he disparages you to destroy your confidence. That way you'll be less likely to attract another guy and may eventually settle for him. If he can't get you himself, he sure doesn't want anyone else to have you.

This qualifies as abuse. No matter how "funny" he thinks he is, if it's hurtful, and you've told him so, it's out of line. Your first line of defense should always be to shut him down completely by ignoring him. If ignoring him doesn't put an end to it, talk seriously to a teacher or coun-selor. Everyone has the right to be comfortable walking around in her own life without fear of bullying and harassment. Don't put up with it.

Hi Meg,
Congrats—I heard that you finally got Rick-o the sick-o (or Dick-and-he-is!) to stop pestering you—that's very good news. He was way too creepy. And speaking of creeps . . . Something kind of funny happened

on the way home from school today. This guy comes up to me and says, "Do you want to go for a pizza and then get naked with me?" I couldn't believe it! I managed to choke out a "NO!" so he says, "What's the matter, you don't like pizza?" What a loser—does he really think a line like that would work? As I'm walking away, he's still hard at it, yelling to me that his other car is a Jaguar, and that he's a champion weightlifter. As if that stuff would make me want him more!

Later,

Tara

The Whole Truth, and Nothing but the Truth

The smitten teenage male is often guilty of embellishing his personal history, all the better to impress you with, my dear. You know the little white lies we mean—exaggerations that are completely transparent to girls, but are seemingly believable to guys, despite the fact that they break a few basic laws of science.

How is it possible that:

* At five foot six inches tall, you must look *down* when speaking to a man who claims to be five foot eight?
* He struggles under his load of schoolbooks, yet actually benches 200 pounds?
* He hasn't shot into outer space if he constantly breaks the sound barrier while driving at breakneck speed?
* He's an all-star player of every single sport?
* He needs to shave twice a day when there's never so much as a hint of a whisker?

You're pretty lucky he's set his sights on you, honey! Generally speaking, these are decent, honest boys who just go a little overboard because they want you to like them. Remember, in prehistoric times, these feats of manliness would surely have impressed your female ancestors. If your admirer has been exaggerating the truth, and you kind of like him, why not give the guy a break and go along with it? One day you might just want him to turn a blind eye to a few little white lies of your own. Besides, he's competing, remember. As he's fanning his impressive tail feathers—or belching in your face—just tell yourself it's a compliment. Really.

So Why Would You Want One?

Good question! There's an easy answer. You don't have much of a choice! In the most basic sense, nature commands you to go forth and multiply. For humans, that usually means finding someone to love. It's a very powerful drive and, for the most part, resistance is futile.

> Hey Meg,
> I fell in love this morning! The cutest guy I've seen in like, forever, showed up at school today. His name is Ian and he just moved into the neighborhood. He's in my math class and at lunch Terri told me he doesn't have a girlfriend. I think he might have been checking me out in the cafeteria. Now I have a reason to wear my new skirt tomorrow.
> Tara

Come on, admit it. You love boys. They're like naughty kids. You'd never put up with a girlfriend who acted the way most boys do. If your girlfriend said she'd call you and didn't, you'd be annoyed. If she teased and insulted you, you'd soon lose interest in her company. And if she blew a few loud raspberries in class, you'd think she'd lost her mind. Funny how we have different standards for the guys in our lives. We let them get away with murder, if we like them.

Imagine what your life would be like if every single night, you ate a plain ol' hamburger for dinner. Then one night, someone hands you a bowl of extra-spicy, blast-your-bra-off chili. Suddenly, your eyes water, your forehead starts to sweat, and your tongue feels as though you've burned a hole right through it. It's a punishing meal, but who knew food could taste so good? Even when the chili starts to do a bit of a rumba in your stomach, you might be rather tempted to have yourself another bowl.

Guys are like the bowl of chili you love and fear. The fact that they're so different from us is very compelling: there's the voice, the body hair, the height, the flat chest, the rippling abs (in movies, anyway), the straightforward way of looking at life. Well, we could go on, but you get the picture. The attraction is less what you have in common, than what you *don't* have in common.

Guys provide you with a different–some would say alien–view on life. You'll see things you would have overlooked without them. They'll even force you to see yourself differently and laugh at your hang-ups (we all have them). Since they don't spend all their time trying to be charming and romantic, when they make the effort, it's a rare treat. Strangely enough, your girlfriends can heap all the sympathy in the world upon you, and it won't fix you up and make you feel better the way a few well timed insults from your beloved can! Boys have an uncanny instinct that allows them to be sweet even when they're being total brats, which explains some of their appeal.

I'm really self-conscious about my nose. It's just too big for my face–even my nostrils are too big. My boyfriend thinks I'm crazy for going on about it. He just tells me to shut up and then he starts to make fun of me. One of his favorites is to agree with everything I say in such a way that I end up laughing at myself. One time he agreed that my nostrils were big–huge, in fact. He said a small Austrian village could hide out quite comfortably in just one of them. I know he is just kidding because he always goes on about how pretty he thinks I am. Thanks to him, I don't care about my nose anymore. Maybe it's not so big, after all. Or maybe it is, and I just don't care!

Electrical Overload

There's nothing like the high you'll feel when you know you've made a connection with a guy. When he smiles at you in that special way, it's like having 1,000 volts of electricity blast through your body. It's easy enough to explain it in scientific terms simply by mentioning the hormones we blame for everything. Although that basic drive to go forth and populate the planet can be frustrating, hormones make the effort *so* worthwhile!

When there's love (or at least infatuation) in your heart, everything in life seems brighter. It's like switching from black-and-white to technicolor in an instant. You are jolted awake in the morning and your whole day has fizz to it. And when it goes—sometimes just as suddenly as it came—it's as if a fire just went out and you're standing there shivering and totally stunned. You'll know you're recovering when you start (defiantly) telling your friends, "I like not being crazy for a guy. I don't even want to be involved with anyone." You'll even mean it at the time. Then—BAM! And before you have a chance to say, "Oh, no, not again," you're at the edge looking down into the abyss. The question is not *if* you will go over, but *how*. Will you slip gracefully over the side or do a running cannonball? Your choice, chickadees, but into the abyss you will go.

Scientists, philosophers, and poets have tried for a long time to identify what that feeling is all about. Of late, scientists have said that love is simply a chemical reaction in the human body designed to get us to pair up and have children. They say it only lasts two or three years, just long enough to ensure the deed is done. Maybe so, but the fact that plenty of old couples out there still dote on each other suggests otherwise.

In the end, there's not a lot of romance in analyzing the chemistry of love. Maybe that's because if you examine "the spark" too closely, you end up snuffing it out. Some things are better left alone. So sit back and enjoy. The electricity that you feel in the beginning of a relationship is something to savor. It may well blossom into something stronger, like love, and that can feel pretty wonderful too. But mature love requires a lot of work and maintenance if you want to keep it strong. With the early sparks, there's freedom simply to enjoy the fact that the one you're warm for is warm for you too. There's no other way to feel that kind of combustion!

Hey Meg,
The coolest thing happened today. Ian walked me to my locker after math, and when we got there he started wrestling with me to steal my books. He ended up sort of holding my hand. He didn't let go for the longest time and he just looked at me with this really warm look in his eyes. Oh my God!! My heart is still pounding just thinking about it. It was one of those truly great moments, you know? Now if I could just get him to ask me out . . .
Tara

chapter five

The Chase Begins

*T*he decent guys out there are often too nervous to come over and ask you out "cold," so you need to create a warm, inviting environment for them. Let them come over and bask in your sunshine, Sunshine. Furthermore, you must manage the situation so that the object of your affection actually thinks it was all his idea in the first place. In the end he will be very proud of his ability to win such a prize.

What we're talking about here is the fine art of flirting, a time-honored tradition for getting a member of the opposite sex to notice you in a nonthreatening way. It's important to let that cutie know that you are warm for him without bashing him over the head with a club. Subtlety is the key here.

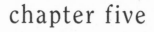

How Are Your Flirting Skills?

Before you read any further, take this short quiz and see how sharp your flirting skills are.

1. You are walking down the hall with your friend when you spot the object of your desires coming toward you. You've never spoken to him before. How do you get him to notice you?

    a. You get so freaked out when you see him walking toward you
       that you start to panic, so you slouch, look down, and try to
       hide behind your friend as he passes.

    b. You wait until he passes and then have your friend yell his
       name. When he turns around, the two of you start to giggle.

    c. You stand a little taller, walk a little prouder, and when he
       catches your eye, you give him the slightest hint of a smile.
       Then you look straight ahead and keep on walking. And swing
       those hips just a bit now, girl, because you know he's turned
       around to watch you go.

2. **It's study period and you see him headed for the library with
a computer sciences book under his arm.**

    a. You watch him through the glass and swoon. When he settles
       down with his nose in the book, you press your nose to the
       glass window and fantasize that you are inside with him.

    b. You follow him in there and offer to help him with his research.

    c. You run back to your locker, grab your own computer sciences
       book, and settle down nearby. You start flipping the pages
       back and forth and look puzzled, as if you don't quite under-
       stand the contents. He might offer to help you.

3. **You are out of school in a social setting and you bump into
the guy you've been mooning over all semester. He's there
alone and you are with a group of the girls.**

    a. You tell the girls how much you are hurting for this guy, yet
       when they invite him to join your group, you are so embar-
       rassed that you leave.

    b. You approach him with the girls in tow. They circle him and
       listen in while you question him about everything—from his
       name to his relationship status.

    c. You find an excuse to break away from the girls for a few min-
       utes, so that he'll see you're alone and won't be too shy to
       come up and say hello.

4. **One of your friends happens to know the guy you've got a
crush on. She introduces you and leaves the two of you**

alone to have a chat. Since you've been doing a little "research," you actually know quite a bit about him already.

a. You can't think of a single thing to say to him. And before he can open his mouth you've bolted away, convinced that he wouldn't like you anyway.

b. You admit to your sleuthing and tell him that you've discovered you share all the same musical tastes.

c. You subtly steer the conversation around to the topics that you already know will interest him. Once you've got him yakking, you just listen enthusiastically.

So, how are your flirting skills? If you've chosen:

Mostly *as*: You'd better look up the word *flirt* in the dictionary, because you don't seem to have a clue about what it means. You've got to be *in* the game to win it, sugar, and you're not even close to the stadium. You need to get yourself some flirting lessons, pronto. Ring up some of your friends who seem to catch the boys they go after, and pick their brains. They would love to help you out and they will be flattered that you are asking for their assistance. Take courage—it's not that scary (and take note of the tips that follow this quiz).

Mostly *bs*: Are you crazy? You are like a runaway train speeding towards Desperado Mountain. The only thing you're flirting with is disaster. Lay off the caffeine and get a grip. You need to look up the word *subtle* because its meaning is clearly eluding you. Tone it down, or you risk being used—or worse, laughed at.

Mostly *cs*: You have definitely mastered the fine art of flirting. Please, share your strategies with those who really need your help.

Flirting is a noncontact sport. It's supposed to be fun. You've got to have a little confidence. One of us was a very accomplished flirt, while the other needed some training. The big difference? Nerve. The good flirt was willing to put herself out there and give it a try. Yes, there were many times when her efforts did not bear fruit. There's always the possibility of rejection, but the only person who needs to know what you're up to is you. If you flirt well, it's so subtle that no one could actually call you on it, so denial is easy. Like he can prove you smiled at him ever so slightly! Flirting is not teasing. It is just a hint of interest and you are under absolutely no obligation to buy the merchandise if it doesn't hold up under closer scrutiny.

Meg! Help!
I have got to get Ian to ask me out on a date. I keep seeing him in the halls and we say hi, but we're not exactly moving forward. I feel I was way too obvious about my feelings for Josh and that just got me burned. How did you get Bryan to ask you out?
Tara

No worries, Tara.
I am a master of asking guys out without actually asking them out. In fact, I've never really asked a guy out. No matter what they say, I think guys still kind of prefer to do the asking. As for Bryan, I just flirted with him constantly until he finally cracked and asked me out. It's a good way to avoid complete rejection, I figure. So start batting those lashes, baby. I'll call you later with some tips.
Meg

Have Patience

If the object of your desire repeatedly "misses" your signals, he's either not interested or not in the market at the moment—or dense! Generally, if you make eye contact and the guy turns away, it's pretty obvious. It doesn't mean he necessarily finds you unattractive, but he isn't receptive to your charms. You may want to try again in case he's the shy type; but after that, throw in the towel. There are plenty of fish in the sea, so don't waste your energy on the wrong one.

On the other hand, flirting can be a long process. You can't just try it once and sit back waiting for results. The amount of time that you'll need to put in before your cutie works up his nerve to ask you out will vary from guy to guy. Give him time to get used to the idea. You definitely need patience to catch your prince the subtle way.

It can be frustrating to pursue the object of your desires slowly. In fact, it's almost painful to wait for him to make a move when all you want to do is make him your boyfriend *now*. But your patience will pay off in the long run, we promise. When you manage to catch a boy this way, he ends up believing that he was the one chasing you all that time. And since he believes he's put in such an effort to capture your heart, he will value what he's caught. A boy who values you will treat you very well indeed. And hey, you're worth it!

Doing the Legwork

Of course, to put all those flirting tips to good use, you'll need to get within striking distance. Perhaps the gods will smile upon you and drop the object of your affections directly into your path one day. Maybe you'll even be wearing your favorite outfit when it happens. Some people are born lucky, but most of us have to work hard for our luck!

To improve your odds of experiencing the "chance" encounter, you'll probably have to do some work up front. You can start by thinking about where you might casually run into your cutie. This is the ideal opportunity to showcase your finely-honed powers of deductive reasoning. Yes, you'll need to study, but this type of research is highly entertaining and you'll never need to crack open a book (unless it's one of his favorites and you're looking for clues). Your mission, if you choose to accept it, is to learn enough about your guy's interests, through observation alone, to: a) determine if you have anything in common; b) gather fodder for the conversation you will need to initiate eventually; and c) make *educated guesses* as to where you might "bump into" him.

It's all about paying attention to detail. If you both attend the same school, keep your eyes open and you may see a pattern to his schedule. He's carrying a hockey stick on Tuesday morning? Where's the ice, Sherlock? He's heading towards the music room at 4? Check out the next school concert. Just remember to keep a low profile: the point of this exercise is to have fun and get a guy to notice you, not to make him uncomfortable. If it occurs to you that you're being too obvious in your research efforts, you probably are. As always, respect is the name of the game.

Tips for Successful Flirting

1. *Let your body do the talking.* There is nothing more attractive to others than a person who exudes confidence. Even if you aren't feeling it inside, you can fake it on the outside. Lift up that chin. Stand tall and put some attitude into your stride. Set yourself apart from the crowd and he will notice you. Other nonverbal signs of interest include tilting your head to one side, shrugging, tossing your hair, and massaging your hand or arm. All of these are viewed as welcoming gestures by the opposite sex. (They work on you, too!)

2. *Look friendly.* Slap a smile on your face that will show a guy that you are approachable and won't reject him. If you don't know each other yet, you can work up from the smile to an enthusiastic "Hey! How's it going?" next time you see him.

3. *Make eye contact.* Guys will always take it as a positive sign when you catch their eye. When you are chatting to your friends, just shoot a friendly glance his way every now and again. Don't overdo it. Leave the steamy eye-lock in the romance novel.

4. *Give him a chance to approach you.* If you constantly surround yourself with a flock of chicks, no guy will have the nerve to approach. Make it easier on him by finding ways to "bump" into him when you're on your own.

5. *Don't wait around too long.* Keep it moving. There is a difference between giving him a chance to catch you on your own and waiting around like a lost puppy. Let him see you having fun with your friends. Guys are attracted to girls who are independent.

6. *Send in the girls.* If you've been in the same room for ages and he still hasn't approached, have your friends start chatting up his friends. Before you know it, you'll be face-to-face with Mr. Maybe.

7. **Be agreeable.** Once you have the chance to talk to your crush, don't freeze up. Make it as easy as possible for him to chat to you. Ask about his interests or ask for some advice on a school subject. Give him the opportunity to feel like an expert. (You know how they love that!) Whatever remarkable feats he describes, admire him a little.

8. **Laugh with him.** If he says something funny (intentionally), laugh sincerely. Don't start braying nervously, but make it clear you find him entertaining. If you're quite a comedienne yourself, tone it down. No matter how witty you are, this isn't the place to showcase it.

9. **Pay him a compliment.** Nothing over the top here, just some little thing that will make him feel good. Tell him you like his shirt or his cologne. One nice comment is enough to encourage him.

10. **Be confident.** You don't need to be perfect to attract a guy; you just need to be sure of yourself. Concentrate on what you are saying so you won't come across as giddy or wishy-washy. Brains are sexy.

11. **Try the "accidental" touch.** Once you get to know him a little, it's time to send out a few more signals. Lean in when you talk to him and try to make some kind of brief physical contact. Grab his arm for a split second while you laugh or make your point by tapping on his knee. It may seem cheesy, but it works. What you're doing is giving him the sign that he might just be able to win your heart, that you might "choose" to spend more time with him.

12. **Take 'em one at a time.** Pace yourselves, girls. Target one guy and stick to that guy until it's run its course, for good or for ill. Don't veer off track the second some new cutie catches your eye.

On the Move

Tear yourself away from your computer or telephone for awhile and get out there and play. Prince Charming will never ride into your backyard on his white charger and knock at your patio doors. Take that as a given. We know it's tempting to hang out in the usual places so that your prince can easily find you, but believe it or not, you'll improve your chances of making that first connection if you're constantly on the move.

Get involved in activities. Now, that doesn't mean joining a community baseball team if you loathe sports simply because he might end up playing at the same park on the same night. It has to be something you enjoy. Surely you have some interests that overlap with his (you'd better!), and you can capitalize on those. Say you're both big fans of music: try joining a band, or getting a part-time job at a local music store. You're animal lovers? How about volunteering to walk the dogs at the local shelter? The bonus here is that whether or not you ever run into him, you'll feel good about what you're doing and you'll meet people who share your interests.

It almost goes without saying that you must share this mission with your girlfriends. Then, when you're out doing whatever you usually do together, whether it's seeing a movie, playing road hockey, or hitting the mall, several sets of eyes will be on the watch for that guy. Nothing brings girls closer than sharing a common goal. You will remember the fun you had in the research long after the your crush is history.

One last word of advice: be patient. Even in a big city, where it might seem like you're looking for a needle in a haystack, you can locate your guy. He's out there somewhere. In fact, he's probably out having fun with his friends and they may "accidentally" stumble upon you first!

Hey Tara,

Thanks for including me on your little adventure to try and run into Ian. I had a great time, but then I always have a great time at the mall. I thought we'd hit the jackpot with that lookalike in the CD store, but when I saw he had Britney Spears' latest in his hand, I knew it couldn't be Ian. She's not his type – <u>you</u> are! Well, better luck next time. Maybe he'll be at the rink on Saturday night.

Meg

Yikes! There He Is!!!

Ultimately, if you're out there doing your thing and keeping your eyes wide open, your mission will be successful. Be prepared for the "chance" encounter. Dream up a rough idea of what you could talk to him about. You don't want to sound like you're reading from a script, but you should be ready with a few topics to fill in any awkward silences. Whatever you do, remain calm and remember the tips for flirting: stand tall, exude confidence, be friendly, make him feel comfortable, and let him know in your own subtle way that you are interested in him romantically. Now, go get him, Tiger!

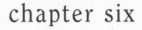

chapter six

Did I Just Say That Out Loud?

*D*o you ever become a blithering fool in the presence of a male you just want to jump all over? Do you find yourself wondering what evil presence has taken over your body, turning you from the charming, self-possessed Dr. Jekyll into the stammering, vacuous Ms. Hyde? Welcome to the club, gals! We all have a drooling alter ego just waiting to make an appearance at the worst possible moment.

When that special guy comes into view, you may experience a temporary meltdown. You'll know this is the case if:

* Your knees go weak.
* Bats swoop around in your stomach.
* Your mind goes blank.
* Your mouth goes dry and your tongue feels as though it's the size of a watermelon.
* Your face burns.
* You suddenly understand why they make adult-size diapers.

You will definitely create a lasting impression in this state. Unless your guy is trained in first aid, he'll likely walk off with a puzzled look on his face to tell his friends about the freaky little thing who cornered him in the hall and froze. Very few teenage boys are together enough to be able to put a petrified gal at ease.

What brings on a meltdown? We'd like to tell you that it's a curse from beyond, but the sad truth is that we bring it on ourselves. It comes from spending a little too much time in fantasy land. You know what we mean, ladies. You can admit to us that you romanticize aspects of your life. Have you ever progressed through an entire relationship in your head, before you even meet the guy? Welcome to a normal day inside a girl's mind. Why nature has seen fit to wire girls this way is beyond us, but it is undeniable that most of us build intricate fantasies around guys we admire. You don't have to know a thing about him for this to be satisfying. In fact, it's easier to "create" his personality, without inconvenient reality getting in the way.

It all starts innocently enough. One morning, for example, you stop into Starbucks on your way to school. Behind the counter is a very attractive guy wearing the name tag "Justin." You order a cappuccino, and Justin expertly steams the milk and pours just the right amount into the espresso. He smiles at you as he hands it over and suddenly, you're in Luv. The next day you go back. And by the fourth day, he's putting extra foam on your cappuccino because you've become a "regular." One day you notice (by practically crawling over the counter to get a closer look) that the fingernails on his left hand are shorter than those on his right and you realize that he must play guitar. In fact, you suspect he's a very talented musician. The next day you hear him singing along with the background music and you are sure of it. And now that you know all about Justin, you begin to have a "relationship" with him in your mind:

You begin by "chatting" about his music, his upcoming CD and his dreams of being a rock star. You're there for his big break, for the start of the world tour, for the feature in Rolling Stone. *Then you're on his arm (wearing a fabulous dress) when he wins the Grammy Award. Shortly after this, he proposes to you one night on stage and slips a diamond ring the size of Texas on your finger. But then it all starts going downhill. The music is getting in the way of your relationship. And what about that clingy backup singer who gyrates against him during his shows? It's almost a cliché. You start making demands, but he just gets more and more distant and your heart is breaking when . . .*

"Would you like cinnamon or chocolate on your cappuccino?"

What?! Oh. You're in the line at Starbucks. And you're definitely having a meltdown.

Nothing is crueler than reality breaking into a rosy fantasy, but that's what happens when lover boy steps out of your mind and into the school hallway. Guess what? He's not a prince, or an actor, or a rock star (yet!). He's not necessarily kind, or honest, or funny, or creative—at least you have no concrete evidence to support your theories. All you have is the makings of a fine screenplay, with all the clever dialogue, the conflict, the love scenes. You've been developing a fictional character very carefully, by building up layer upon layer of detail.

By the time you actually meet him, the whole thing might be played out. When the real guy opens his mouth, it can cause a weird collision of fact and fiction. Oh my god! He's nothing like I imagined him at all! Now, it's often surprising how accurate we can actually be. As a rule, girls are careful and consistent observers, and that helps you make logical leaps in building up a character. But still, the reality can be a major disappointment.

Meanwhile, Back on Earth

Do guys play out these scenes? Maybe they do, to some degree, but it isn't along the same grandiose lines, judging by what they tell us, anyway. We gather that there are mental movies going on, but they tend to be X-rated. And basically, they have no idea what remarkable scenes we play out in our romantic minds. They're just going about their lives, eating, sleeping, and playing, completely unaware that we're setting up remarkable fantasy challenges for them, so they can prove themselves worthy of our company. Most guys would be embarrassed to discover an admiring lady has ascribed wonderful traits, motivations, and actions to them.

So what's to be done if this is all very common and natural? Well, the best way to keep yourself from building a fantasy he can never live up to is to meet him as soon as possible. It's much harder to put him into an imaginary romantic comedy, when you already know he's cowboys and horses all the way. It's also a good idea to accumulate as much real information as you can, so you avoid filling in the blanks with myth.

And finally, the best thing you can do is to keep yourself so busy that the only time you have for such creative work is five minutes before falling asleep.

The Five Ps (Proper Planning Prevents Piss-Poor Performance)

Pull yourself together and chill, baby. Take courage from the fact that he doesn't know what you've been thinking. Keep in mind that he might have given you a thought or two as well. No, it won't be the stuff of myth and legend. And it might not be the stuff of centerfold fantasy. But even guys have moments of romantic sweetness:

> When Mark was 14, his brother came running down the stairs one morning and announced, "So who's Elizabeth?" Mark almost choked on his bran flakes. "How did you know?" he said, wondering if he'd yelled her name in his sleep, or if one of his friends had turned him in. His brother grinned and explained. Mark had written the name of his lady love in the steam on the bathroom mirror after his shower. The steam had disappeared by the time he left the room. But when his brother took a shower, the name reappeared on the mirror in the fresh steam, exposing his crush to the cruel eyes of an older brother!

After you've taken a deep cleansing breath, you're going to have to make like a Boy Scout and be prepared. Sooner or later, you're going to talk to Adonis. Call it the law of averages. If you follow him long enough, one day he'll turn around and say hi. Don't make the mistake of assuming that you'll be able to think on your feet. You won't. To make a good impression, you must be yourself and you can't be yourself when you're all wound up.

The key, as usual, is to rehearse. Decide ahead of time what subject matter you can cover on your "chance encounter." Some guys might be good talkers, but most will rely on you to get the ball rolling. So play out a *realistic* conversation in your head. Don't get bogged down in specifics, because it will never go exactly as planned and you don't want to freeze just because he doesn't get his "lines" right! Just work through some general scenarios so that you'll have some boundaries when you speak in person. It will help prevent you from coloring way outside the lines.

Smooth Talker

It is critical, when you are chatting up a boy, to remember that he *is* a boy. That means he *thinks* like a boy, so you don't want to talk to him in the same way you'd talk to a girlfriend. Girls appreciate knowing all about a person's deepest thoughts and feelings. Guys don't. They live in a concrete world where they discuss *things*—world news, music and sports scores—not emotions. They need to be very comfortable with someone before that can happen, and comfort doesn't grow in five minutes in the school hallway.

This doesn't mean you can't talk about the crazy math teacher you both have. He'll enjoy hearing some funny stories about the guy. What he won't enjoy is taking a walk with you into the Girl Zone of pop psychology where you analyze that teacher's motives and speculate on what happened in his past to make him so weird.

Since there is so much dangerous water to avoid, have a few boy-friendly topics in mind. You can always start by asking him about his school subjects. Ask him if he's into any sports. (This also provides you with additional information on where he might hang out after school.) Talk about a few Web sites you think he might like. Ask if he has a part-time job. Does he have any pets? Has he seen the latest action movie?

In fact, this is a classic opportunity to employ the "non-ask out, ask out." Select a movie that all the guys have been raving about and ask him if he's seen it yet. If he hasn't, he'll probably say that he wants to and then of course he'll say, "Have you seen it?" It doesn't matter if you have or not. What you say is, "No, I really want to. But all my friends went while I was away one weekend, so now I don't have anyone to go with." If you've chosen a cutie with half a brain, he should be able to pick up the ball that you've just slammed into his court, and suggest you see the movie together. If he misses this huge hint, don't give up yet. He may just be so nervous talking to you that his receptors are in a fog.

Stay Focused

Remember, guys love to talk about themselves. (Who doesn't?) So you just need to introduce a topic, ask a few questions, and get him going. Sometimes you'll hit a topic that's a dud—it'll start to sound more like an interrogation than a conversation. So the more topics you have ready, the better. It is imperative that you get him talking, because the more *he* talks the less likely *you* are to suffer from a sudden and severe case of verbal diarrhea. That's what happens when you get so nervous about facing an awkward silence that you launch into a stream-of-consciousness monologue, rambling on about anything and everything that comes to mind. When you finally slow down to take a breath, you might find your cutie doing one or more of the following:

- ✳ Looking confused and afraid
- ✳ Checking his watch
- ✳ Mumbling about "needing to be somewhere"
- ✳ Looking around desperately for someone to rescue him
- ✳ Slowly, almost imperceptibly, backing away from you

If you can check off even one of these signals, you're in trouble. The goal here is to convince him that you are interesting and easy to talk to, not a raving, self-absorbed lunatic. You need to leave him lingering, wanting more, not smoking up his Nikes sprinting away.

Meg help!
You're going to laugh when you hear what I've gotten myself into this time. I saw Ian today and I managed to stay calm enough to talk to him. Actually, I was doing great, asking him all about what he likes to do and it turns out he's really into long-distance running. Before I could stop myself I said, "Really? I love running too!" Me, the queen of the couch potatoes, telling the guy I lust after that I can actually run. But wait, it gets worse. He says, "Since I'm still new in the area, maybe we could go running together sometime and you could show me some good routes." "Sure! I'd <u>love</u> to!" I say. Oh, why did I say that? HELP! Now what do I do?
Tara

Compromising Your Principles

Once you're on speaking terms with your hottie, you may start to hear some strange ideas coming out of your mouth. When a girl has it bad for a guy, suddenly her interests may closely resemble his. How many of you have feigned a love for sports just to win a few points with a new boy? And that's just the beginning.

I had this major crush on this older guy in my neighborhood. I was friends with his sister so I had talked to him a couple of times. One day he told me what his favorite book was, so I haul off to the library and check out the book. I spent the rest of the summer rushing home to sit in the big tree at the bottom of my driveway. I would sit there on a branch and read the book (which was totally gory and disgusting—all about these soldiers in Vietnam) in the hopes that he would walk by on his way home and see me there. I felt like such a loser because I never saw him and I couldn't even understand the book. What a waste of a summer.

I had it so bad for this guy that when he offered to cook me his favorite hamburgers, I quickly accepted—even though I hadn't eaten meat in a couple of years. If that's all he could cook, I decided I could choke one down. I figured he was special, and I could forget about the cow who died to make it happen. In fact, I think I liked him enough that if he'd suggested we eat an endangered species, I would have offered to get the forks.

Don't Go Changin'

Although stories like these are harmless enough, remember that when you are pretending to be something you're not, you will be uncomfortable because you're in unfamiliar territory. And if you get caught in the lie, it will be embarrassing because he'll know you've got it bad for him. You don't want to give him this advantage over you. Besides, he'll wonder why you can't just be yourself.

It's fine to show interest in his stuff, but never at the expense of your happiness or self-respect. Go to his hockey games once in a while if it's important to him, but don't become the team mascot and freeze your

True Confessions

- Have you sat through a movie that was so gory you'd already refused to see it with your friends?
- Have you wasted a Saturday afternoon watching a wrestling match and memorizing some of the wrestlers' names just so you could slip them into casual conversation with him later?
- Have you bought a CD of a band that you absolutely hate, just because he loves it?
- Have you declared your love for swooping down the ski slopes when you hate the cold and are afraid of heights?
- Have you offered to walk his dog even though you're allergic?

butt off at 10 P.M. twice a week just to win his heart. Some things just aren't worth winning!

As a teen, it's sometimes hard to believe that the person you are is interesting enough to attract a guy. You'll just have to take our word for it that it *is* enough to be yourself. You don't have to have everything in common to make it work. Some of the happiest couples we know don't share any interests at all, except for their interest in each other. While being yourself is the single most important element in attracting boys to you, we do know that it can be incredibly difficult to relax and just do what you do. You don't need to change to get him to like you. Think of all the people who already like you the way you are.

If you haven't already noticed this, you will likely find that you become infinitely more interesting to other guys once you have a boyfriend. Is this because guys like girls with boyfriends? No. It's because guys are attracted to girls who are confident—and girls who already have boyfriends tend to be more relaxed and natural around all guys because they are no longer out to impress. The tricky part is holding onto that feeling when you become single again. It's not impossible.

Anyway, don't sweat it if you don't have everything in common with the guy whose heart you're trying to win. There will very likely be enough common ground to get you started and maybe you can develop a few interests together. And if you don't share his interest in monster truck rallies, by all means say so—he'll expect it!

Tara,

I can't believe you're going to take up running! Ha! Ha! You're gonna
die, sister. I can try and help you "train," but I don't know how much
you can accomplish in a week or two. Next time you should just tell
him a bunch of us are going out somewhere and invite him along. Then
give me a call and we'll throw something together. But to make you
feel better, before we were dating, I told Bryan I loved hard rock and
he still plays it for me all the time. I'm getting deaf thanks to that
little white lie!

Meg

Who'll Crack First?

You've chased him all around town for a month, you've been utterly
enchanting, and you've thrown more hints than confetti on a new bride.
If there is any justice in the world, the guy will finally ask you out!
Unfortunately, there are few people more oblivious than the teenage
male. Shifting gears from friendship to a romantic relationship is tough
and your honey may lack the social savvy to carry it off. After all, he's
just as vulnerable to rejection as you are. It may be that no matter how
much he likes you and how much encouragement you've given him, he
just can't do it. Better to keep things as they are, he figures, than risk
losing your friendship altogether.

In military circles, this is known as a deadlock. Each side has taken
a position and neither one is budging. The game cannot continue unless
someone makes a move. You have three choices at this point: (1) you can
stumble along as you are (if you can stand it) in the hopes that he'll
finally crack; (2) you can work up your nerve to move things along a
little; or (3) you can crack yourself and take your chances on asking him
out directly. We favor option 2, although we'll understand if you're frustrated enough to take the plunge and go for 3.

When fear is holding your little chicken back, the only way you are
going to get him to make a move is to give him a firm push on his feath-
ered derrière. If you wait much longer, the buzz will wear off or one of
you will get scooped up by another who's bolder. Without further delay,
you must hit him up with the nondate date. This means you'll invent a
transparent and lame excuse to get that boy alone for a few hours and

convince him that you're destined to be together—for a date or two, at least. Don't worry, *you'll* know the excuse is lame, but Chicken Boy won't. If he hasn't picked up on the hints you've sprinkled like bread-crumbs in his path, do you really think he's going to be suspicious when you ask him for help with your history homework? Please! Trust us when we say that your fine-feathered friend won't sense the setup.

Mind you, your excuse has to be somewhat convincing, so you won't laugh as you say it. There's no point in blowing the game now that you've come this far. Just tap into something he likes to do:

✳ Most guys have some knowledge of techie stuff, so ask him to help you buy a new Walkman, a new program for your computer, or a video game.

✳ If he's into sports, ask him if he'd mind coming with you to select a tennis racket that has the right grip for you. Then hit him up for a free lesson.

✳ Maybe he could help you select a new snowboard or mountain bike.

✳ If you can get your mitts on some tickets to a sporting event, tell him they were a gift from your friend but now she can't go. You'd hate to waste them, so would he like to join you?

✳ If cameras are his thing, tell him you promised your mother a framed shot of her beloved Barky as a birthday gift. Could he help you line up a few shots and maybe walk you through developing them in the school darkroom?

Come up with an excuse that will help signal interest, not pressure. Keep things light and casual. If you are feeling too shy to do this in person, e-mail him. What you definitely *don't* want to do is have your friends ask him. He'll certainly feel pressured then and may freak out and deny being interested. Never underestimate the viciousness of a chicken. Many a nice girl has been pecked to death and there's no glamour in it.

All you're aiming for here is one-on-one time with him doing an activity that will distract him and soothe his jangled nerves. Guys like to have a reason for getting together or a task to perform. His confidence will increase dramatically as he performs a service for you, because he wants to prove he's a good guy.

When you have his attention, and everything is going well, then hit him with "the follow-up." How rude it would be to accept his help without thanking him properly! So, after the repair job, offer to take him out for coffee or a bite to eat as a gesture of thanks. When you're at the burger joint, you'll have time for a real chat. The "follow-up" is like a date without the pressure. You'll get a better sense of whether there's any point to pursuing the hunt to its inevitable conclusion. You wouldn't be the first girl to find that the hunt is better than the catch. When you're staring at your prey cramming fries into his mouth and talking with his mouth full, you may just decide to move on to a new target. On the other hand, if you both nurse your coffee or sodas for an hour or more, chances are you have enough in common to proceed into the real date phase.

Strength in Numbers

Organizing a "group date" is also an excellent way to break a deadlock. It's simply a matter of choosing an activity everyone can enjoy and seeing that your guy gets invited. Group dates really help take the pressure off both of you. When you're in this setting, you'll automatically have something to chat about that puts you both at ease and others will help keep the conversation flowing. Besides, each of you will take courage from the support of your friends who are standing by and thinking, *Will the two of you just go for it already?* The girls will make sure you have time alone to chat by taking off, and dragging all the guys with them. Here are a few suggestions to get you started:

* Try a night at the bowling alley. Everyone will laugh at the nerdy shoes and a competition of girls against boys will stir things up.
* If the weather's good, go out to a park or conservation area for a day of hiking or cycling together. Everyone can bring something for a picnic lunch.
* Take a good rock-climbing lesson.
* Visit the nearest amusement park, fall fair, or indoor video-game facility. Make sure you're standing beside your guy when you line up for the rides.

* Check out a go-cart place. Watch your honey drive like a maniac to impress you.
* In the summer, head out to a waterslide park. In the winter, meet at a skating rink, or head to a nearby hill with your toboggans.

Meg,

Thanks for your idea about that group date, but Ian's beaten us to it. At least, I think he has. He has asked me to help him pick out a gift for his parents' 20th anniversary. We're meeting at the bus stop Saturday morning to go to the mall. What do you think? Is it a date?

Tara

P.S. I hope this means I won't have to do any more running!

It's Enough to Make Your Head Spin

Keep your eyes open, because you might not be the only one using advanced techniques. Sometimes, Chicken Boy will turn the tables on you. Instead of asking you out on a formal date, he'll slide the ball into your court by asking you on a nondate or a group date.

One of the most frustrating situations in the early stages is determining whether both parties consider it a "real" date. All you can do is look for the signs and hope for the best. It looks promising if he:

* Made some effort to plan for the "date"
* Smells better than usual
* Teases you more than usual and nudges you around just to make physical contact
* Mentions how nice you look or tells you your hair smells great
* Leans toward you when he talks to you
* Sneaks a look at you when he thinks you won't notice

If you can say yes to a few of these, chances are good that Chicken Boy is discovering the rooster inside. On the other hand, it's definitely a bad sign if he:

* Looks as if he just rolled out of bed
* Blatantly checks out other girls

✳ Refuses to come out of his way to meet you or walk you home
✳ Won't meet your eyes or isn't listening to you
✳ Leaves a vast space between you as you walk together

If you need to answer yes to more than one of these, your chicken just isn't trying hard enough to impress you. Call Colonel Sanders.

The Other Boy

One thing that might throw a little wrench into the works is that other boy. What other boy? We're talking about the other boy who's been standing on the sidelines while you try to figure out where you stand with Chicken Boy. Chances are that you've had a special glow lately. You've worked up a heat pursuing your prey and you're having fun. Boys are attracted to girls who seem fun, and from where your new mystery boy is standing, that looks a lot like you. Maybe he'll surprise you and ask you out point-blank!

Now what do you do? It's time to weigh your options. Take a closer look at what's really going on with Chicken Boy. If you've tried the non-date and group date options and things still aren't progressing, it may be time to move on. At least you know where you stand with the newcomer. Don't risk missing out on something that has potential just because you've invented some imaginary "commitment" to Chicken Boy. You could hang around for years (and many women do) on just the faintest hint of interest. Forget about it. The hunt is fun, but you need to know the catch is within reach.

Sorry, Charlie

On the other hand, if things really are starting to sizzle with Chicken Boy, or the new boy just isn't your type, it looks as though you'll have to do the brave and merciful thing and turn your admirer down as gently as possible. Remember, he has paid you a compliment just by asking for your company. You owe him your respect, even if you think he's the nerdiest guy in school. Spare him his dignity and thank him for his offer. Tell him you are flattered by his interest, but you've just started to see somebody else. That way, he can blame it on bad timing. Even if you aren't seeing someone else, there's no excuse for treating someone badly—or killing him slowly by avoidance and subtle hints that you aren't interested.

The graceful decline is one of the most difficult things to master in the wonderful world of romance. In a perfect world, all the right guys would ask you out and all the wrong ones would spare you—and themselves—the misery of the turndown. It just doesn't work that way, and regrettably, you will sometimes have to hurt someone's feelings.

Keep in mind that guys usually appreciate a direct approach, and will take a simple "no thank you" as explanation enough. Do not offer a long list of excuses that suggest doing your homework or visiting your

The Wrong Ways To Turn Down a Guy

- Avoid his calls or his e-mail.
- Say hurtful things (e.g., "You've got to be kidding.")
- Mumble something about being busy.
- Flirt with someone else in front of him.
- Suggest one of your girlfriends might be better suited to his personality (He didn't ask her out!).
- Pretend you're not home if he calls (by pretending to be your sister, or bribing your brother to lie).
- Say yes at first, then call at the last minute to cancel.

There's no grace in any of these solutions, and we guarantee you'll be sorry you used them. Yes, we know it's tempting to avoid an awkward situation, but it's not the way to go. If you want anyone to trust you with his heart, you are going to have to prove that you know how to handle one. The decent guys will find out that you are brutal at rejection soon enough and won't give you the chance to get near them. Have some class, and recognize that someone's interest— wanted or otherwise—is a gift. You may choose not to accept it, but you must respect the good faith in which it's offered.

great aunt are preferable to spending time with him. Just say, "I'm sorry, I can't. But thank you for asking." That's enough for most guys, take our word for it. He'll be grateful that you don't drag it out. Even if you don't sound very convincing, he'll consider he's expressed his interest and leave you to follow up if you'd like another try. If he persists, you can add, "I just want to be friends." That's as far as you should ever need to go.

Unfortunately, some guys will persist even after a polite decline, and then you'll have to be brutally honest. Do not put up with someone who forces his attentions on you or embarrasses you. Be polite, be clear, be firm. A no is a no is a no. Don't give him false hope through vagueness, like "I'm not in a good place to date right now," or "I'm just too busy." The truth is, if you were interested, you'd make the effort and you'd make the time. Spit it out so that the air is clear and you can both move on. It's definitely harder at that moment, but so much better in the long term. If you're honest and decent, he'll get over a turndown and be comfortable as your friend.

Taking It on the Chin

Here's an unpleasant bit of news for you: No matter how positive the signals are that he likes you, there's always a margin of error when it comes to guessing other people's feelings. There's always a chance that he'll say "no thank you" to your overtures. Obviously, the more groundwork you've done and the more positive feedback you've received, the fewer the chances of getting shot down. But there are no "sure things" in romance.

It takes a brave person to make the first move toward intimacy in a friendship. If you take that first step and you're met with rejection, it's not the end of the world. It's just the end of your chances for romance with that one guy. For the moment, it hurts—particularly if you've invested a lot of time and energy into pursuing him. But be honest with yourself, you had fun in the chase, didn't you? Lots of times, it all works out beautifully. If you go for it and you are rejected, at least you tried. If you don't go for it at all, you'll just never know, will you?

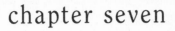

chapter seven

The Big Date

*C*ongratulations! You've earned a graduate degree in flirting, and you're a champ at getting the nondate date! All of your hard work has paid off and you've got yourself a real date with that guy.

Meg,
IAN CALLED!!!! We had a great talk and he said he wants to thank me for helping him shop for that gift for his parents and did I want to go out with him next Friday? His dad gave him two tickets to a basketball game. A real date! I can't wait! What should I wear? How should I do my hair? I want to look good—but not like I've put any effort into it. What happens if we don't have enough to talk about for three hours?
Tara

If you are nervous about awkward silences on your big date, then do a little prep ahead of time. Think up a few questions that require more than a yes or no answer. Once you've got him talking about his interests, one thing will lead quite easily to another. Even with guys, conversations tend to go off on tangents, far from the original point.

It is a two-way street, however. He will need to carry his weight too. You can do your part to encourage him just by showing interest in what he's saying and asking for more detail. If you are "right" for each other (for now!), it won't be hard. If you're not, that will become evident by hour 3 of your date when the well has dried up. But that's what dates are all about. It's a job interview. You're trying to learn more about each other to discover whether each of you is right for the "job" of girlfriend or boyfriend. If he's not right for the job, it's no big deal. There are plenty of other willing candidates.

Meg to the rescue!
That's great news! Ian is such a cutie—way to go! A basketball game could be fun. You don't want to look too dressy though. Why don't I come over and bring along my lucky T-shirt—it's what I wore on my first date with Bryan (and believe me, that was a <u>great</u> date!). I'll drop by tomorrow after school.
Meg

75 Hours, 30 Minutes, 20 Seconds, and Counting . . .

For you, half the fun of dating is in the buildup. For the lucky guy . . . let's just say he sees things a little differently. To illustrate, we'll take a look at how the scene might play out as "D-day" looms.

51 hours

You . . . call in your chief advisers to review your clothing options for the big date. You combine their stuff with your own and put on a fashion show while they lie on your bed.

He . . . is playing basketball with his friends. He has not mentioned the upcoming date.

27 hours, 42 minutes

You . . . are staging mock "date" conversations with your friends that test your ability to run with difficult subjects (e.g., fly-fishing, baseball stats, African insects).

He . . . is playing video games with his friends. He still hasn't mentioned the date.

19 Hours, 13 minutes

You . . . are completely unable to focus on your homework. You have sent 12 e-mails to the girls to get their input on various worries.

He . . . checks to make sure he has a clean shirt, then sits down to finish his homework, tunes blaring.

3 hours, 23 minutes

You . . . race home after school for the do-it-yourself spa treatment.

He . . . is finishing a game of pick-up basketball and heading over to get a burger with his pals. When they suggest a movie later, he says he can't–he has a date. The guys tease the hell out of "lover boy."

1 hour, 10 minutes

You . . . have laid out the 13 different makeup products you need to create that "natural look" guys love, and begin to apply them systematically. You carefully blow your hair dry.

He . . . is watching a *Baywatch* rerun.

28 minutes

You . . . try on three different tops and two pairs of jeans before going back to the "approved" outfit.

He . . . checks his watch and decides he has another 10 minutes.

12 minutes

You . . . notice that your hair has a kink–a ridge, really–that's appeared out of nowhere. There's a sudden flurry. Hair clips are flying. Panic is setting in!

He . . . throws on the clean shirt.

7 minutes

You . . . are gelling the hell out of your hair and it's stiffer than a helmet. You hope your date won't get a splinter if he touches it.

He . . . is walking out the front door with his father.

2 minutes

You . . . are satisfied that the hair's okay, then almost burst into tears when you notice a blemish.

He . . . arrives on time to find you calmly opening the door looking fabulous.

The Moral of the Story

The prep is for you. It's not that it's wasted on the guy, per se. He'll appreciate how good you look, no question about *that*. It's just that he'll think you look great if you just shower and walk out the door. He wouldn't have asked you out if he weren't already attracted to you.

That's how guys work. If he likes the way you look, he's usually willing to take a chance on your personality.

Most girls operate a little differently. If someone asks you out and he's not the hottest guy on the planet, you might still say yes. If you like his personality, you're willing to take your chances on the attraction. You'll get to know him a little better. If he's funny and decent and smart, you'll likely become increasingly attracted to him until you actually decide he's the cutest guy in the world.

It's tempting to think guys are the same, but it just ain't so. Simply put, if he asked you out, he thinks you're shaggable. Even if he later decides that he doesn't like your personality (impossible, you charmer), he'd probably still agree to a good shagging (not that you're offering). You, on the other hand, would be appalled at the very idea if you disliked him. As we've said before, ladies, guys are just wired differently. So, don't worry too much about how you look. Doing the spa thing can be fun and will make it feel like a special occasion. It's pure self-indulgence and it may help you feel calmer and more confident. But you're not doing it for the boy.

Which brings us to another point. When he pays you a compliment such as, "You look great tonight," just say "thank you." If you respond by laughing or saying, "You must need your eyes checked," he may decide that complimenting you is the wrong thing to do and you sure don't want him to think that. Guys are afraid of seeming lecherous and they don't always know how far to go in admiring you. Rest assured he wouldn't say it if he didn't think it. Enjoy the moment—you DO look great.

No Big Deal

So, should you be insulted that he isn't building up a pre-date frenzy? Nah. It's just one of those basic truths of life: no matter how hot that boy may be for you, he won't put much energy into making himself more attractive to you. He figures clean is good enough—and he isn't far wrong, is he? This doesn't mean he's not interested in you. It just means that . . . well, he's a *guy*, that's all it means. It's not because he's less excited about the date than you are.

Okay, maybe he is. Teenage boys don't place quite the same importance on having a girlfriend as teenage girls do on having a boyfriend. They like girls, but they like a lot of other things as well—football, cars and big screen TVs. They also like to spend time with their buddies and they really care about what those guys think of them. The guys would never be impressed to hear he'd spent time worrying about how to dress for your date.

Girls would do well to follow the guys' example. It's all about balance. While you think he's totally awesome and you love spending time with him, you need space in your life for lots of other things (like the girls, music, chocolate, and interesting conversations and ideas). Having a boyfriend is cool, but it's not the single most important thing in life (really!), especially for teenagers. You don't want to make the mistake women used to make of getting so caught up in another person that you forget about developing yourself. While you can have some terrific times with a guy, make sure that you can also have a terrific time *without* one. That way, you won't waste a minute of your life wishing away the time until you have a boyfriend.

R-E-S-P-E-C-T

When you do decide to spend your time with a boy, make sure he's worthy of your company. You need to know that his interest in you is sincere and that he isn't using you for anything. You need to be 100 percent sure that he respects you and that you can trust him. How will you know? It helps if you already respect yourself. Recognize that you're number one, sister. You're busy, you're bright, and you're talented, and he's damn lucky you can make room for him in your schedule. Isn't that the story you want to be telling? You should never sacrifice yourself to attract or keep a boyfriend, because in the long run, it doesn't work.

If you make it too easy for a guy, he may just take you for granted. To recognize your worth and appreciate how lucky he is to have you around, he needs to work hard to gain your approval. If you're making life simple for him, he'll slack off. That's not just a guy thing—it's human nature. We value what we work hard to win. Don't offer up everything. You must leave him wanting more.

Here's a news flash for you: If you're dating a guy and he's treating you with disrespect, you have no one to blame but yourself. That's right, it's all *your* fault. You need to set standards for yourself and others by demanding respect and appreciation. If you aren't being treated properly,

Have A Life

- Don't sit by the phone. If you need to go out, go out. If he misses you, he'll try again later.
- Don't put him before your other commitments to your pals, your schoolwork, your job, your other interests—it's all important.
- Don't hold off on making weekend plans. If he hasn't asked you out by Thursday, make other plans. Spend your time with those who value it—like your girlfriends.
- Don't play games. Be straight. If he waits too long to ask you out, make other plans. Don't just say you did, get out and enjoy yourself without him.
- Don't do too much for him. Don't give him Hershey's Kisses every week, knit him a sweater, or offer to do his schoolwork. If you have this much time, you'd better find something else to fill it!
- Don't be jealous. You must be confident of your own charms. If he gives you reason to be jealous, why waste your time with him?

MOVE ON. No matter how hot this guy is, no matter how much you like him, you should dump him if he doesn't treat you well. If you want a boy to cherish you (and who doesn't?), then you must abide by a few simple rules.

Go with the Gut

You will have some fabulous dates and you will have some hideous ones (that subject could fill a whole book). But most will fall somewhere in between. Your intuition will usually give you a clue about whether to see him again. There's nothing wrong with going on a second date even if you're not convinced it's going to work out. Sometimes it takes a few encounters to get a clear decision. You will, however, want to avoid saying yes when you're certain there's nothing there. If your gut is screaming "run," don't say yes just to delay hurting him. Over time, you'll develop a good sense of who's right for you. Eventually you will settle for nothing but the best. You'll be surprised at how many guys will value your company and how well they will treat you to keep it. Expect a little more, you'll get it. And be prepared to walk away when you don't.

chapter eight

Hot Lips

You must remember this,
A kiss is still a kiss,
A sigh is just a sigh.
The fundamental things apply,
As tongues collide.

So what's the big deal about kissing, anyway? Two people press their lips together, so what? When you look at it that way, it's hard to understand what's so romantic about a smooch. But when the right two people are pressing lips together, it becomes an incredibly intimate act. The humble kiss, a hint of acts of greater intimacy, is very satisfying in and of itself.

On the tension scale, the end of the first date ranks pretty high. You'll be thinking, *Does he want to kiss me? Will he try? Do I want him to? Should I go for it myself just to break the tension?* It's nerve-wracking for both parties. You each will be trying to gauge not only your own desire to press lips, but the other person's as well. If he doesn't, he may not be really interested. On the other hand, maybe he's so interested that he's too nervous to try!

To make it even more complicated, you may find that although you had a great date and you like him, the thought of sealing it with a kiss just doesn't appeal. Attraction is a complicated thing. There is no explaining why we prefer one person to another. It defies logic. Say you've talked for hours with the cutest guy in the school and you're thrilled by how much you have in common. By any measure, this was a good date. And yet, to your surprise, you find you'd just as soon shake hands when he walks you to your door. Two weeks later, you could go out with a guy who's a bit low on charm and no hunk of beefcake, and yet you have an unaccountable urge to lunge across the table at him and silence his silly comments with a lip lock. Go figure!

First Contact

Is he going to kiss you this time? How will you know? Will he be any good at it? Will *you* be any good at it? How far wrong can you go? What if you screw it up, will he laugh at you? Talk about anticipation! You end up standing there, waiting for it to happen, and trying not to *look* as if you're waiting for it to happen. Inevitably, you become increasingly nervous and either bolt away, just to break the tension, or worse, start babbling to fill the gap.

God only knows what's going on in a guy's mind during this time. He certainly knows you're *expecting* it, but he has his own demons. In the end, what should be simple and straightforward is not. There you are, dying for him to do it, searching his body language for any hint of an impending kiss, trying to give the right signs yourself while maintaining a certain nonchalance. You noticed he popped a mint 10 minutes ago—that should be a good sign—and he keeps shuffling his feet and hanging around. If he didn't want to, he'd just leave, right? Oh, wait, that looks like a head tilt . . . He's leaning forward—YES! YES!! Ladies and gentlemen, we have contact!

Those of you who are old pros in the kissing arena will already have discovered that the first kiss is not always quite what you'd imagined. Most of us tend to picture something along the lines of those big Hollywood screen kisses. In the movies, it's always clear that a kiss is approaching. The two stars exchange smoldering glances as the background music swells. He leans in at the exact moment she tilts her head in anticipation and boom—he brings that baby in for a smooth landing. What we tend to forget is that these kisses are *staged*. Every move is carefully choreographed to look perfect. And still, the kiss that makes the final cut probably took half an hour to get just right. What you never see are all the takes where things weren't so picture perfect. Just as it happens in real life, of course.

Even if you've had a lot of practice, when you kiss a new guy for the first time, there might just be a head butt if the angle isn't quite right or both of you lean to the same side. And how about the smashing of noses or bashing of teeth, which *could* spell the end of romance but never do? You'll laugh and try again and the next one will hit the mark.

The Politics of Smooching

Given all that's wrapped up in a simple kiss, it's no wonder it doesn't always happen on the first date. You might go out several times before he works up the nerve to try and you work up the nerve to receive. He, too, can get caught up in worrying about all that can go wrong. What if, horror of horrors, he decides to kiss you and you turn to give him your cheek? To him, that's the "kiss of death." Generally speaking, if you refuse the lips, he'll be discouraged and see it as a refusal of intimacy with him. On the other hand, if he takes the safe route and deliberately goes for the cheek, don't be alarmed. He's usually just working up to the real thing.

Check out the signals you're giving him. You may think you're looking entirely confident and composed, but you may not be coming across that way. Are you looking down or away from him out of nervousness? Remember that guys are not overly gifted at reading your expressions. What he should read as nervousness, he may well see as disinterest. If you sense he'd like to but isn't, you may need to give yourself a pep talk. Take our word for it, it's nearly impossible to screw up a kiss. The worst that can really happen is a lack of coordination, so relax. Instinct will kick in soon enough and you will do fine.

The French Connection

Somehow, the kiss always lands safely and perfectly if you're *not* attracted to the guy. Without jitters, it can be big-screen-perfect every time—but why bother? A kiss without romantic interest is a soulless thing. In fact, if you truly have no interest at all in the guy with whom you're locking lips, it can be kind of unpleasant. *My god,* you'll think, *I don't want to do this. I hope he doesn't—Yuck!* When you're not hot for a guy, the notion of having his tongue waving in your general direction is kind of . . . disgusting. It's a *tongue,* after all. It belongs in his mouth, not yours.

Remember back to when you first learned there's more going on in a kiss than the meeting of lips? Did you find the prospect appealing? Not likely. And even though you know what to expect, it can still come as a shock the first time it happens. It's just *weird!* What's weirder is how darned enjoyable it is with the right guy, especially when you're completely comfortable with him. If you're really attracted to a guy, "gross" is the last word you'd use to describe what you're doing.

The Bad and the Ugly

Now, as we've said, kissing is largely an instinctual ability. The downside is that some guys just have bad instincts! They'll go ahead and kiss you even when you're doing your best to send out very clear "Don't you dare" signals. If you don't want it to happen, rest assured, there won't be a moment's hesitation on his part. It's just one of the ironies of life.

What about the guy who, despite all opportunities to plant a few on you privately, prefers to get a little action in the school hallways, the mall, a friend's party, or the video arcade? Keep in mind that smooching is generally interesting and enjoyable only for the happy couple involved. This is supposed to be an act of intimacy—and intimate means private and personal. Take it home! If one of you feels compelled to indulge in major PDAs (public displays of affection), it usually signals a lack of confidence—a need to "prove" to everyone that you're his and he's yours. That's not romantic; it's needy. There's nothing wrong with a kiss or two in public. But if your tonsils are in danger of slipping from their rightful positions, you'll hear the sound of flushing and there goes "class" down the toilet.

Be on the lookout for potential hickey situations. Even the sweetest of kisses can end in purple bruises that are somehow seen as reflections on your character. Hickeys are very easy to come by and very hard to disguise. There you are in the middle of a delicious clinch and suddenly Count Dracula has taken over the body of your guy. He's attached himself like a vacuum to your neck and in seconds, a large bruise has formed. Don't overestimate the effort it takes. Incidentally, we have yet to see one on a guy and we suspect some of them do it deliberately as a form of "branding." You are nobody's heifer, Betsy, so don't let him treat you as part of his herd.

Fortunately, raunchy kissers are few and far between. You can expect that most of your kisses will be pleasant experiences both for you and the guy. Just keep those lips kissable and well lubed with gloss or balm. And to make sure your breath won't kill, keep on brushing those pearly whites and floss, floss, floss. Heaven forbid you should leave a piece of last night's fish dinner wedged in there for him to discover after 24 hours of decomposition. While you're at it, give your tongue a good brushing with your toothbrush, too. If you've taken all precautions, you'll be fully confident heading into the clinch. That way your mind will be free to think only of how great it feels to be kissing that special guy of yours.

chapter nine

So, You've Got a Boyfriend (This Week, Anyway)

*T*hat guy of yours is definitely *all that*. He's cute and sweet and considerate and reliable, and he treats you better than a platinum credit card. The only problem is, he hasn't asked you to be his girlfriend yet.

If only all the cutie pies out there would get straight to the point and ask, "Do you want to be my girlfriend?" It doesn't get much clearer than that, but those words don't spring easily to a guy's lips. The word *girlfriend* screams of "commitment." And commitment says "trapped" and trapped says "death is near." Exaggerate? Who us? Never. You'd be surprised how closely the words *commitment* and *death* are located in the lexicon of a young male. *D* comes right after *C*, right?

You could grab your honey by the hand and say, "Are we officially an item or not?" On the other hand, you could take a needle and plunge it into your eye. It will be no less agonizing than watching your guy writhe in pain as he weighs his affection for you against his fear of commitment. Do you really need to see this?

Number One Guy?

Why not try doing it our way first? It's easy and it doesn't require throwing yourself upon your own sword. All you have to do is take a good look around you. Do you spend lots of time together? Do your friends call him your boyfriend? Do his friends consider you a couple? Does he remember to call when he knows you've had a stressful day? Yes to all? So far, he's looking a lot like a boyfriend even if it's not official.

Keep in mind that "boyfriend" is just a word. If it looks like a pig and oinks like a pig, it's probably a pig. What difference does it make if you go out with "Wilbur" on Friday night, or "my boyfriend Wilbur" on Friday night? Okay, maybe it does make a difference in the level of confidence you feel in the relationship, but Wilbur is still Wilbur whether you slap a label on his forehead reading "Boyfriend" or not. In the early stages of a relationship, you must accept that there's going to be some gray area.

Be very cautious about discussing your "status." Nothing will send a boy running faster and farther than saying, "We need to talk about our relationship" or "I need to know where I stand with you." This somehow is processed through his simultaneous translation device as: "I've chosen my wedding dress."

It's only natural that you'd want some reassurance that he does consider this an exclusive relationship. But now that you know how easily guys spook, maybe you could hold off on getting the formal title until you hear *him* use it. Often you will first hear it in passing, as if it just slipped out by accident. One day, a friend of his will walk up to the two of you and he'll introduce you as his girlfriend. Maybe he'll tell a story about wild times with the guys and add, "but that was before I had a girlfriend." That's the sort of thing you're looking for. "Offhand" is a guy's preferred way of doing business. You'll see this a lot with that boy of yours. He will make some surprising assumptions and just slip them into conversation, because the other "c-word" that he hates as much as *commitment* is *confrontation*.

If the situation is really bugging you, you could try making some passing, casual comment about a future event to check if he's thinking about you in a long-term way. For example, if it's October, you could say that you are hoping he'll teach you a few new snowboarding moves this winter. You'll know he considers you his main squeeze when he responds to your future plans with enthusiasm. And unless you've been dreaming up all the attention he's been giving you lately, he will definitely respond with enthusiasm. It looks as though you've got yourself a boyfriend, girlfriend!

A Few Pointers

Since you've volunteered to immerse yourself in the company of a male, it might be helpful to examine what makes these dudes tick. Understanding how different they are will keep you one step ahead of trouble. You might be able to put out any flames that could become nasty forest fires. Here's what Smokey the Bear's girlfriend would want you to know:

1. *Guys will open their mouths in their own time.* If they are pushed, they will clam up. Worse, they may tell you something that you don't want to hear. As you get to know each other better, and he feels more comfortable, you will be pleasantly surprised to hear all the sweet things your baby has to say about you.

2. *Speak now, or forever hold your peace.* If he has done something to hurt your feelings, speak up. He might make the mistake of treating you as he would his guy friends, and may not realize he has hurt your feelings. For example, if he called his friend a moose, that wouldn't bug the guy.

3. *Say it fast and keep it simple.* For example, instead of telling him about how you were chubby as a child and it's affected your self image, just say, "I don't like being called a moose." Case closed. He will appreciate your directness and will assure you that he would never call you a moose if he thought you'd take it personally (go figure!).

4. *Don't invite him to analyze your life.* If he doesn't enjoy analyzing how *he* feels, analyzing how you feel is probably not his idea of a good time either. Leave this to those who thrive on it—your girlfriends.

5. *Accept him as he is.* It is insulting to him if you try to change the basic qualities that make him the fabulous guy he is. A wise man once said, "Never try to teach a pig to dance. You'll only end up frustrated and you will piss off the pig."

6. *Resist the urge to solve his problems for him.* We know you mean well and he does too, but if something is bothering him, he may not want your help. If you don't push, he may open up in his own time. Then just stuff a cork in your mouth and listen. If he wants your advice, he'll ask for it.

7. *Give him space.* Your guy's friends will put pressure on him if he starts spending too much time with you. He needs time to hang with his pals. And that doesn't mean you can tag along. Don't be a cling-on.

8. *Leave the past behind.* Don't start yapping about your last boyfriend. Do you want to hear about his ex? And don't try to boost your profile in his eyes by telling him about other boys who like you. That's kid stuff.

Meg

I had the best time with Ian yesterday. I went to a family barbecue for his dad's birthday. His dad is hilarious, by the way, and told me all about the cute things Ian did when he was little. I don't think Ian was too amused though. Anyway, we had a great time. He held my hand— in front of his family—and when his dad dropped me off at the end of the night, he walked me to the door and kissed me good night. Then he thanked me for coming and said, "It's the first time I've ever invited a girlfriend to a family dinner." I just said, "No problem"—and tried to keep from cracking a huge grin. I'm so happy! E-mail soon.

Tara

He's Starting to Bug Me Already

Meg,

I need your advice. I've been Ian's girlfriend for a whole week now, and yesterday I think I panicked or something because all of a sudden when I was talking to him, I noticed how big his ears are. This never struck me before, and god knows, I spent enough time staring at him. I was trying to block this out when he started to joke with me about our science teacher and he just seemed a bit goofy all of a sudden. For a second I thought I didn't like him any more and I feel bad because I think he noticed. I'm not sure what happened to me—did you ever have doubts about Bryan?

Tara

Hey Tara,

Are you kidding? I still have doubts about him all the time. I think it has something to do with deciding not to see anyone else. That's a big deal you know. Don't be so hard on yourself. Ian is a really great guy and you'll get used to the idea he's your boyfriend. Really!

Meg

If you experience a few bumps along the road to love, don't panic. It doesn't mean things are over. You're just in an adjustment period. Although some girls are able to leap right into a relationship without so much as batting an eyelash, others need to proceed with more caution.

Besides, it's pretty natural to experience a bit of a letdown after the chase is over. You've caught the guy and things are settling down. It's great, right? Right, but it's also a tiny bit disappointing. It's amazing how you can be so enthralled by how cute he is one moment, only to re-think the whole thing after you see him dance. Yikes! You never realized he could be such a dork.

Fortunately, he need never know you're having second thoughts. He might be facing down a few of his own. Just take a bit of a breather and let yourself settle into the new situation. When you've been off the roller coaster of courtship for a spell, you'll learn to like the calm again, and you'll really appreciate the fact that some guy finds you attractive and charming and funny day after day.

There will be rough patches, that's for sure, and we'll give you the same advice we give each other: Take it easy—and keep your expectations low. Sit back and think about whether he's the problem, or whether it's your thing. Do not expect a guy to know what you need all the time, or create confidence in you that was never there before. Romance is a wonderful thing, but it's not a magic bullet.

In the meantime, give that new fellow of yours the benefit of the doubt. Remember all the reasons you were attracted to him in the first place. Don't start looking for faults, and don't make him prove himself over and over. Nobody's perfect, including you! Be proud of your guy and be proud of yourself for attracting such a good one.

Spoiling Your Guy

You and Mr. Right-for-Now have been getting cozy for a while, and you're probably feeling as though you want to do something nice for him. Finding the perfect gift for a guy is tough. You want to give him something he will like and you want it to be original. You want it to say enough, but not too much. And, most important, you don't want it to be too expensive. Love does have limits!

Here are some suggestions to get you started in the search for the "perfect gift":

1. **His and hers**. If he has a pierced anything, you can buy a pair of earrings. Give one earring to him and keep the other for yourself.

2. *Time for you.* A guy can always use a snazzy new watch strap. Maybe he'll think of you whenever he checks the time.

3. *A tube of designer hand cream.* Tell him you want soft hands to hold. Corny, but he'll love it.

4. *Cool shades.* A person can never have too many pairs of cheap, funky sunglasses.

5. *Music man.* If your guy plays an instrument, buy him some sheet music (maybe for a song that you both love), or a new set of strings for his guitar.

6. *Comic madness.* Maybe he likes to sketch comic book characters. If so, he could probably use some new sketching pencils or erasers.

7. *Shutterbug?* Give your favorite photographer a roll of film and a coupon for free developing or a cool picture frame.

8. *A gift certificate to a music/video store.*

9. *Specialty magazines.* Choose one that concentrates on your guy's interests (a race car or motorcycle or movie mag).

10. *Mountain biker?* He'd probably love a water bottle to attach to the bike or a tire pump or some cycling gloves.

11. *Totally tapped out?* Make up some coupons that he can redeem for one free neck massage (your hands, of course) or a one-time cleanup of his locker.

12. *Flick tickets.* Give him some vouchers to see some movies.

13. *A Boy Scout?* Check out army surplus stores. There are lots of inexpensive utility knives or cool mini-flashlights on the market that your Boy Scout would love.

Tara
Well, I decided to go the traditional route with the anniversary gift for Bryan (partly because it saved me some cash.) What can I say? I picked up some heart-shaped cookie cutters, and I baked him some chocolate chip cookies. They turned out really well. I even dipped the bottoms of the hearts in melted white chocolate. I hope he likes them and he'd better not forget to give me something!
Meg

Items to Avoid

- A man's purse
- A "how-to" video of the latest dance moves
- A subscription to *Groom* magazine
- An extra-small jock strap
- Love poetry
- Tarot cards
- Anything in a basket

A Really Big Night

If you want to treat your guy to something special, why not totally spoil him for one night? Take him out and do it up big, from start to finish. You could take him to see the latest play or musical. Get the discounted student tickets for a matinée performance. Then buy him a funky daisy boutonniere or a box of chocolate cigars, and pick him up at his house. After the play, treat him to some ice cream or café au lait, and be sure to walk him home and end the date with a kiss at his front door. (Unless it's getting late, in which case, he should be walking you home.)

It's fine to buy your guy a gift once in a while, but don't shower him with baubles. He'll appreciate it—and you—far more, if it's an occasional thing. Make sure you let him know you appreciate everything he gives you. One girl we know even managed to seem thrilled when her beau gave her a baseball glove for Christmas, followed by a physics book for her birthday. You may not see the logic in your boyfriend's gifts— after all, flowers aren't expensive and they're always welcome—but he's usually trying. Rave over the great ones and smile bravely over the failed attempts. Let him spoil you a little, and then, every once in a while, show him that you're thinking about him.

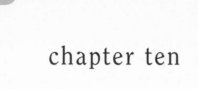

chapter ten

The Wild Thing

*D*o you ever get the feeling that each and every teenager in the world is having sex—except you? You hear about it on the six o'clock news, you read about it in the headlines, you see it on your favorite TV shows, and it's staring at you from the magazine racks. Everyone is doing it. Really. Life is just one long orgy for teens and you're invited. We'll agree there's some pressure on you from the media, boys, your friends, even from yourself. If you're not shagging madly, what's holding you back, sister? Do you want to be the last virgin in this solar system? Will that be your claim to fame?

Oh puuuleeezzz! Nothing could be further from the truth. It reminds us of that famous quote by Mark Twain: "The rumors of my death have been greatly exaggerated." Well, the rumors of rampant teen sex have also been greatly exaggerated. Yes, plenty of you are having it, but plenty are not. Given that there's almost 20 million of you in the United States alone, we'd say those of you who aren't having sex have lots of company. Take a really good look around at all the teens you know. Are they really "getting it"? Or do they just want to? Or do they just *think* they want to? We'd go so far as to say that most guys really do want to; but with girls, the matter is a little more complex.

Obviously, at this time in your life, there's a lot of sex-charged chatter going on inside your head and out. It can be tough to sort out what's right for you. We understand how difficult it is to stand up against the crowd when you don't want to join them, especially if that crowd includes a beloved boyfriend. And if you really do want to, who are we to stop you? Well, we're not even going to try. If there's one thing we've learned, it's that nature will have her way with all of us. Might as well try to change the course of Niagara Falls!

What we are trying to do is slow you down. Why? Look at it this way: People have very little control over a lot of things that happen in their lives. First, our parents make all our decisions. Then by the time we can make our own, we have to take into account work, rent payments, boyfriends, partners, kids, mortgage payments, health—and fate. The decision about when, where, and with whom to have sex is one decision that you really do have complete control over, so you might as well consider it carefully.

If You Had the Chance to Do It All Again

What we do want to say is that it is a big step, and it is a big deal, and you will think so later if you don't think so now. Worse, you'll recognize how big a step it was with great regret, if you don't handle your decisions now the way you'll wish you had. You wouldn't believe how many women we know who rushed into having sex and now try to forget their unpleasant first experience. This is something that you're going to think back on a lot over the next 70 or so years. Do you want to shudder in horror over the memory? If the circumstances of your first encounter are wrong and if you are scared, hurried, uncomfortable, and confused, that's exactly how you'll remember it. Yes, you'll have other, better memories to add to this one, but make no mistake, your first time is the one that will keep springing to mind.

Emotion has a way of engraving an experience on your memory, and there's nothing like a little fear and confusion to carve a moment in time right into your gray matter. One day, a few decades down the road, you'll be stuck in traffic and something will bring on a flashback of that scene—the one where you're having sex for the first time. You'll remember the sights, the sounds, and the feelings as though it happened yesterday. Now, you can either put your head down on the steering wheel and wait for the memory to pass, or you can sit back and smile and enjoy it all over again. Take your pick. Like it or not, you will be creating a memory with your first sexual encounter. Make sure it's one you'll treasure, not one that will make you feel sad, disappointed, or angry. After all, there's only one first time.

Mind you, we're not suggesting that you hold out for the romance novel consummation. You could wait for your prince to ride up on his white charger and slay a few monsters to win your hand. You could keep your legs carefully crossed until he carries you across the castle threshold, tosses you upon a white-canopied bed in the turret, and ravishes you. Sure, that could happen. But waiting for it sounds like something your parents might recommend. As two women who have no vested interest in keeping you locked up till your prince arrives, we're simply suggesting that you take your time. We have noticed that for women, the emotional changes that lay the groundwork for a mature sexual relationship often aren't fully realized until the late teens. For many of us, it's later still. We'd go so far as to say that we've rarely met a woman who's had sex before age 18 and been happy with that decision in retrospect. But we also realize that every girl is different and must make her own decisions about timing.

If you love and trust the guy you're with and you feel completely comfortable with him and with yourself when you take the plunge, you'll have nothing to worry about in the flashback department. You'll set yourself up quite nicely for the satisfied smile in the traffic jam 30 years hence.

Lies, Lies, Lies

"Everybody else is doing it."
"You'd do it if you really loved me."
"I'm going to explode—you wouldn't believe the pressure."
"Guys just *need* it."
"You'll feel better too. You won't be so tense and uptight."

It's easy enough to say no to creeps who throw you a bunch of crap like this. But what if you've been seeing your boyfriend for months and you've become very close and he's starting to put pressure on you? That's where the going gets tough. You love him and you don't want to lose him. And yet you just don't feel that the stars are quite aligned for you to make that move. What to do?

Open your mouth and talk! You've got to be honest with your guy, and tell him how you feel. If you are close enough to be discussing the possibility of sex, then you'd better be able to share your hopes and fears about it. If he's worth including in those hopes, then he'll definitely respect your decision. If you aren't ready for sex yet, he'd better be cool with that or he'll be cooling his heels elsewhere. And the loss will be his!

> Tara,
> I'm so upset. In fact, this is the first time I've stopped crying long enough to turn on the computer. You will not believe what happened today. Remember, it was the big six-month anniversary for Bryan and me? I gave him the special cookies and I made him a card. And what do you think he gave me? A box of condoms! He actually wrapped up the box and put a bow on it. I almost died. It pissed me right off. We've talked about the sex thing before—like 40 times—and I've told him I just don't think I want to yet. Lately he's been getting really pushy and so I'm becoming less willing to consider it. I'm even starting to avoid being alone with him because he won't drop it. Anyway, we ended up having a huge fight and he stormed out. He hasn't called and I'm not calling him. He used to be such a nice guy. I can't believe he's acting like this.
> Meg

Hear Ye, Hear Ye

What if you are truly, madly, deeply in love with this guy, but your gut is telling you that you just aren't ready? It's simple: You're not. So don't do it. But do that guy of yours a big favor, and let him in on what you're thinking. Don't underestimate the drive he's feeling. It's at least as strong as yours, and the big difference is that he's probably willing to put aside all the emotional factors involved in a sexual relationship and just go for it. You probably can't do that. Yet, boys, too, can feel pretty mixed up and insecure about relationships. Throw in some social pressure, and he may get the idea that it's his role to be the aggressor. Even if he's not so sure he wants to start up a sexual relationship, he thinks you expect him to make a move, given that you've been together awhile (and you probably do!). So talk to him and let him know how much you care about him, but make it clear that you're comfortable with things as they are. He may actually be relieved. Even though guys are 10 times more eager for sex (okay, 60), they are also pretty nervous about the whole thing and may be secretly hoping you'll put the brakes on.

On the other hand, if you reject his advances and you don't explain your real reasons, he may jump to the conclusion that you don't really like him that much. Again, you need to open up and share your feelings. You've probably gone further with him than you have with any other guy, so tell him that. Tell him that you're crazy about him and that he'll be the first to know when you're ready to heat things up a bit. If he cares strongly about you too, this should be all he needs to feel more secure about you and he'll relax and back off.

Meg,
I'm so sorry about Bryan's anniversary "gift." It's great that he's obviously willing to wear a condom, but it's too bad that he's getting so pushy about wanting sex. It's so depressing when the good guys lose their minds like that. Maybe his friends put him up to it? Even though Ian and I aren't anywhere near that point, we've already talked about sex. I told him I'm not ready to go there yet and he told me that's fine by him. He is still a virgin too—and says he's in no hurry. I hope he means it. Maybe you should just call Bryan and talk this through?
Tara

Hi Tara,
I just picked up your e-mail and I'm telling you, there is no way I'm calling that creep. I've put the bow from his lovely gift by the phone in case I weaken. I don't have the gift itself, having thrown it at him before he left. Maybe he's sharing it with someone who cares. I shouldn't have to tell him how I feel about this. He should know. The really dumb thing is, that I always thought that he would be my first. I really loved him but I just needed more time. Now I'm glad I never slept with him.
Meg

Is He "the One"?

Let's assume that you and your boyfriend have been going out for months. He's always sweet, he tells you he loves you, and you really love him. You're starting to think he could be your "soulmate" for life. And you do enjoy fooling around with him. Still, you hesitate about taking the next, big step. Maybe you're nervous or scared. Maybe you're worried about whether he'll be able to handle the intimacy of your new relationship. What if he panics and dumps you? Or maybe you're afraid that he'll feel the need to share his "score" with his friends.

When doubts like this are running through your brain, have enough respect for yourself to listen. It's probably your intuition talking. Something isn't quite right. To be able to enjoy sex, you need to relax. If there is a knot in your stomach and a nasty scenario on your mind, you can't possibly relax. Sex can bond two people, but it can also tear them apart faster and more painfully than almost anything else if both partners aren't 100 percent confident and ready to take that step. There are some pretty sad stories out there from those who rushed it.

I'd been seeing Chris for about six weeks. Last weekend, he called me from his cell phone late one night. He was right out front and wanted to come in. My parents were away, which he knew. I let him in and pretty soon we were making out on the couch. Now I knew the guy wasn't head over heels for me, but I really liked him and I wanted it to work. So I had sex with him. He didn't have to force me! It was okay—I didn't see stars or anything. After it was over, he got right up to leave—said his parents would expect him home. I wasn't happy, but I walked him to the door. I leaned over to give him a kiss good-bye and he gave me the cheek. Can you believe it? We'd just had sex and he gave me the cheek. I went back to bed and cried. It's been a week and he hasn't called me, so I guess that's that.

Pressing the Stop Button

It's very easy to become confused when you're in the clinch. When you really care about a boy and you're enjoying a good snogging session, you can soon find yourself beyond the point you'd planned to go. One minute you're doing the tongue tango, the next minute you are proceeding with purpose down that path that has only one destination. Yikes! Getting jiggy with "it" wasn't on the agenda.

You're going to need to rehearse this scene in your head a few times, because you cannot count on the right words coming out of your mouth when the hormonal tide is rushing in. Yes, you're a mature young woman, but you may just have trouble remembering your own name when you two are all over each other. Those crashing waves are very loud, but you must raise your voice above them if you know you aren't ready to take things to the next level. Don't let things go so far that you're afraid your boyfriend will be annoyed with you when you press the alarm. Of course you can always say no. But past a certain point, you can also expect him to be quite frustrated when you do. He's a good guy and he will stop. And because he is such a good guy, you must be fair to him too.

Don't make the mistake of thinking that because it's a girl's right to "just say no" you can continue to make out until you're good and ready to call it a night. That's pretty selfish behavior, and it has no place in an intimate relationship. If you care about your boyfriend, then consider his feelings too and show him the same respect that you demand. This means you don't lead him on. It's unfair and if you keep it up, he'll start thinking you're a tease—and he'll be right.

Taking the mature approach isn't easy. It means you can't get yourself into a situation that is hotter than you can handle. If it were easy, there wouldn't be so many women far older than you who find themselves pregnant—or worse—all because they weren't prepared for things to go as far as they did. Having sex wasn't in the plan, but one thing just led to another . . . Don't be as irresponsible as the grown-ups! Before you start to play ball, make some decisions. How many bases can he run? Tell him, "No home runs tonight, Slugger, or you'll be tossed out of the park." That's fair play.

Running for Home

Be realistic. If the two of you keep passing first base, and you strongly feel that this is someone you are going to have sex with one day, then you need to carry your frank discussion with this boy one step further. Sadly, it's a lot easier to *have* sex than to talk about it, but talk about it you must. So, when you are discussing the possibility of having sex, make sure that what you are BOTH talking about is actually the possibility of having *safer* sex.

We use the term *safer* sex, as opposed to *safe* sex here because the only truly *safe* sex is abstinence (which means no sex at all). There are always consequences to having a sexual relationship with someone. There is the risk of pregnancy and disease. There are also emotional consequences. Sex can change how you feel about yourself and about the person with whom you're involved. Sometimes, these emotions can be very distressing (especially if you've allowed yourself to be talked into doing something that you weren't ready for). If you feel you can't handle these consequences, then you aren't ready to have sex. And keep in mind that you must be prepared to handle them on your own. There are no guarantees that your partner will stick around when the going gets tough.

If you are seriously considering entering a sexual relationship, you owe it to yourself to learn about the risks. No doubt you've already heard in school, or from your friends, that sex carries with it the risk of pregnancy. But how much do you really know about sexually transmitted diseases (STDs)? Did you know that there are more than 25 kinds of STDs? The most common include:

- Human Papilloma Virus, or HPV (a cause of genital warts)
- Chlamydia
- Gonorrhea
- Herpes
- Hepatitis B & C
- Syphilis
- Trichomoniasis
- Yeast infections
- Pubic lice or "crabs" (wingless insects with crablike claws that nest in pubic hair and dine on blood)
- Human Immunodeficiency Virus, or HIV (a virus that attacks cells that have important functions in the immune system)
- Acquired Immune Deficiency Syndrome, or AIDS (Believed to be caused by HIV, AIDS damages a person's ability to fight off disease, leaving his or her body open to attack from unusual types of cancer and ordinarily harmless infections.)

Left unchecked and untreated, these diseases can lead to sterility, liver damage, cervical and liver cancer, painful bladder infections and kidney damage, circulatory damage, heart and brain damage, and in the case of AIDS, even death. What's particularly nasty is that you can have an STD and have no obvious symptoms. This means that you could have a disease and not know it. Or your partner could have a disease and unknowingly pass it on to you.

What's a Girl to Do?

If you know the risks and you still decide to have sex, what can you do? You must INSIST that your partner wears a *latex* condom—no ifs, ands, or buts! Do not assume that you are "safe" because you are using the pill or some other form of birth control, including condoms made from other, natural materials. These things will *not* protect you from disease. And, by the way, you can get STDs and HIV from oral sex as well as from intercourse. The only thing that is 98 percent effective (only abstinence is 100 percent) in reducing your risk of getting a disease is to place a barrier between yourself and the other person.

In the case of intercourse, this means using a latex condom correctly EVERY time. Don't get carried away and take a chance "just this once." Taking that one chance could change your life forever, and possibly even end it. You only need to have sex once to get a disease. Don't assume that your boyfriend will be responsible enough to buy condoms. Of course, he *should* share in this responsibility. (If he doesn't, you might want to reconsider your decision to have sex with him.) But if he doesn't, you must get that protection. If you are adult enough to have sex, you are adult enough to buy condoms. Remember to check the expiration date on the package—they do have a shelf life.

Please don't let anyone erode your resolve here. Maybe he'll tell you that he doesn't need to wear a condom because he is "safe," or a virgin (virgins can still have some of these diseases, like hepatitis), or he doesn't sleep around. Even the nicest and most trustworthy people get STDs. Remember, the danger is that many people who have these diseases don't realize it because they have no symptoms. He may tell you that he doesn't like how a condom feels, that they are "too restrictive" or a real "turnoff." Make it clear that he has two choices: Sex with a condom or no sex at all. Given these options, he'll soon get used to wearing one.

We certainly understand that it can be difficult and embarrassing to bring up these issues, but it will be far more difficult and embarrassing to explain to your doctor that you've got blisters or critters all over your genitals. Not to mention how difficult it would be to tell the next guy you want to have sex with that *you* have a disease he must protect himself against.

Try telling him that you've decided you want to have sex with him because you care for him so much. And since the two of you are so close, you know you can be frank with him about the need to make it safer for both of you. You might be pleasantly surprised to find a conversation like this can create greater intimacy. The two of you will probably feel closer to each other than ever.

We've just provided you with the basics on safer sex in this book. You can get loads of helpful information (including ways to broach the subject of STDs) from these Web sites:

> *www.fda.gov/opacom/7teens.html* (This is also a great site for info on health and fitness concerns.)
> *www.unspeakable.com*

In the U.S., call the national STD hot line at 1-800-227-8922 or 1-888-833-6448. In Ontario, call 1-800-668-2437 or contact Health Canada for the hotline number in your province.

So, have we managed to knock all the romance out of sex for you now, girls? Sorry, but after all, sex isn't just about love and romance. It comes with a lot of not-so-romantic responsibilities. Make sure you are ready to face *all* of them before you take the plunge.

The Last Word

If you've been worried that your boyfriend isn't as crazy about you as you'd like him to be or you're sensing that your relationship is taking a bit of a nosedive, **do not make the mistake of having sex with him in the hopes that it will bring you closer together.** If things between you aren't absolutely fabulous *before* you begin having sex, they will be usually be *disastrous* afterward. Sex changes the relationship and change is always stressful. If you're both committed to making your relationship stronger, you can help each other through these stressful times. But if you aren't totally committed to each other, then the stress will pull you apart.

You can't force someone to love you or want to be with you. If a guy has doubts about his feelings toward you, the very technique you might use to bring him closer is the one most likely to push him away. Yes, he'll be a whole lot closer for a few hours. But after the glow wears off, it will soon occur to him that you are much more attached to him than before and that you expect more from him emotionally. Then watch your honey take off like a rocket!

Teenage guys are going through the same changes in their lives as you are. They are facing a lot of decisions and they're under a lot of pressure to figure out who they are. Although your guy sincerely enjoys your company and he'd sure as hell love to have sex with you, it doesn't necessarily follow that he'll be able to deal with the emotional intimacy that you are expecting from a sexual relationship. Even if you don't *think* you're expecting it, you are—and on some instinctual level, he knows it. Generally speaking, if you have sex with your guy, you will feel more attached to him. These feelings are wired into us. Cave Girl felt the same way about Cave Boy long ago, because sex meant babies, and babies meant responsibility, and responsibility is better shared. Sex doesn't have to mean babies nowadays, but that brain of yours comes prewired. Don't waste your energy trying to bring it into the twenty-first century. Learn to live with what you've got!

A wise girl sets the limits of her own sexual behavior and protects her boundaries against all persuasive voices, including her own. There is an Irish proverb that says: "When the apple is ripe, it will fall."

If you aren't sure you're ripe enough, you need more time up in that tree. So take it. When you are truly ready to fall, you will—and it will be a wonderful landing.

chapter eleven

The Dump Truck: Is That You Behind the Wheel?

*O*ver the past four centuries many have turned to the words of the great William Shakespeare to find meaning in their lives, especially when dealing with life and death, friendship and betrayal, love and rejection, adoring one's boyfriend and then suddenly finding him repulsive. By happy accident, we recently found a rare first draft of the magnificent tragedy *Hamlet*. Unknown to most Shakespearean scholars, in this early version, Hamlet is a woman masquerading as a man, and she's planning to break the heart of her lover. We quote:

> *To dump, or not to dump; that is the question*
> *Whether 'tis nobler in the heart to suffer*
> *His stupid jokes and outrageous taste in clothes,*
> *Or to admit to oneself that this is no longer for thou;*
> *And by opposing, end it? To dump; to leave.*
> *To leave, perchance to move on: aye, there's the rub;*
> *For in moving on what babes may come*
> *When we have made the break with this mortal lump*
> *We now call our boyfriend.*

Beautiful soliloquy, isn't it? No wonder the Brits chose Shakespeare as the most important person in the history of their land. Old Billy knew well this simple truth: It is far easier to get *into* a relationship than to get out of one. You don't know stress until you realize that the feelings you had for your guy have slipped away and there's nothing left. He's the same guy he always was, the one who used to make your heart pound, but suddenly, your heart is lurching and you know it's over.

Well, it isn't quite over. In fact, it's not over until someone says it's over, and that, dear girls, is the tough part. How much easier romance would be if we could just transmit our feelings to someone else in a way that didn't cause them pain. But that is not the human way. The human way is to suffer—to suffer through not saying what we need to say, to suffer through saying it, and to suffer afterward through knowing we have hurt someone whose only crime was to like us too much. Okay, maybe we're being a little melodramatic. It's all that talk of Shakespeare. The fact remains that when the spark of romance dies out and you're left with a heap of ashes, you can't just stand there and ponder it: you've got to communicate the bad news.

Before you do, you'd better take a good hard look at your relationship. Is it really dead, or just resting? Is it possible that you've hit a bump in the road that you're too impatient to drive around? Could it be that you just need a break to regain your appreciation for what you've got? Are you nurturing a vain dream that there's a perfect guy out there? Are you bored with other aspects of your life and blaming it on your relationship? These are common problems when you've been committed to someone for a while. Sometimes, the mood passes and you wonder what you were thinking.

Hey Meg,
Just wanted to check in with you and make sure everything is okay. Bryan must have called by now, right? That was a close call Saturday, when we saw him at the mall. I worried about you all through English today. Don't worry, I didn't miss anything. We're doing <u>Romeo and Juliet,</u> which isn't so bad as Shakespeare goes, but I'm going to rent the movie again anyway to admire Leo DiCaprio. Let me know what's up.
Tara

Hi Tara,
No, he still hasn't called. I can't believe it. I am still planning to dump his ass when he does, but I refuse to call him to do it. Maybe I should

have just walked up to him on Saturday, but I don't think I can do it face-to-face. I'm afraid I'll start crying. I guess I'll just keep rehearsing my "get lost" speech and wait until I get my chance to deliver it. I'd just like to get it over with, though. It's like we're in this limbo land.
Meg

You've Lost that Lovin' Feeling

Sometimes that relationship is dead all right. But do check for signs of life before you go public with the obituary. You'll know you're standing over a cold carcass when most of the following are true:

* You used to love his smile—but now you notice that he could do with a good flossing.
* You used to be transported to another galaxy by his kisses—but now you resent that he had onions with dinner.
* You used to laugh at his jokes—but now you find him childish.
* You used to plan what to wear when he came over—but now you don't change out of your sweats. In fact, you change into them.
* You used to dream about marrying him—but now the thought of a future with this guy has you reaching for the Tums.
* You used to marvel at how fast the time flew when you were together—but now you find yourself wondering what the girls are doing.
* You used to think it was romantic to split popcorn with him at the movies—but now you only notice the noises he makes as he hogs the bag and stuffs his face.

If you've been feeling this way for a while, it's a pretty safe bet that your relationship is terminal, if not morgue-worthy yet. You're going to have to face the fact that you are no longer interested in this guy as a boyfriend. Having a boyfriend should be fun and exciting, not boring and embarrassing. Ask yourself, is it time to throw that fish back? If so, do it before it starts to rot in your hand.

Dump that boy now. Do not drag it out until you meet someone else. If you're already looking around, then you know that things aren't right. This isn't about whether there is someone else out there for you. It's about your feelings for the boyfriend you've got. If you aren't happy, cut him loose.

Another Point of View

Sometimes you'll need a little help from your friends to sniff out the truth. They may be the first to say that you need to do an offload, because they'll often sense your unhappiness long before you do. And they'll definitely notice if your guy isn't treating you right. You'd think it would be painfully obvious to you that your boyfriend has been treating you disrespectfully, but it won't be if he's managed to undermine your confidence.

If your friends come to you with this news flash, listen to them. If only one friend tells you that he's no good, you may have cause to be suspicious of her motives. But if several raise concerns, they probably have a point. Keep in mind that it won't be easy for them to say this to you, and they know they risk losing your friendship by doing so. If you normally trust your friends' opinions, why not hear them out? Then do what Ann Landers always advises: Ask yourself if you're better off with him or without him. If he's not treating you well, he's outta there! You're too smart to put up with that kind of garbage.

The Coward's Way Out

No one wants to break someone else's heart, but the direct approach is always the right way to go. It will be tempting to weasel out of the unpleasant task by trying to force him to do the dirty work. This is a common chick ploy. A girl decides an offload is necessary, but to avoid delivering the news, she morphs into a cold, mean bitch who makes her boyfriend's life so miserable that he leaves of his own accord. She'd rather take the hit to her pride by allowing him to dump her than to do the deed herself.

Withdrawing all kindness and affection from your boyfriend is far crueler than being quick and merciful. And you will end up disliking yourself for doing it. He'll be confused and hurt by your strange behavior. What's more, he may not even get it, thinking it's a phase. Better to think of yourself as Dr. End-It: You're removing your relationship from his life as you would a bandage from his hairy little arm. Are you going to drag out the agony by pulling it off slowly, yanking out one hair at a time, or are you going to tear it off quickly?

As you ponder this decision, consider that some people say that teenage boys actually suffer more than girls when romances end. Hard to believe, right? But boys, as you know only too well, don't have the same intimacy skills as girls, which causes them to fall in love faster and take a breakup harder. They may not show it, but they're feeling it. So be kind.

A Class Act

We'll take a moment here to introduce the concept of "class." It's a word you'll hear tossed around a lot, but it's tough to define. Basically, a classy person has grace, dignity, and maturity. People are always happy to see her arrive and sorry to see her go. It isn't as hard to attain class as it sounds, because it comes back to the same old rule: treat people just as you'd like to be treated.

If ever a situation required class, the breakup is it. And yet, it's so difficult to have grace and dignity when you are telling someone to hit the road. The problem is that when the feeling is gone, you panic and want out fast. This person you used to like now makes you extremely uncomfortable; and yet he hasn't changed, so you feel guilty. He's standing there with his heart on his sleeve, and somehow you actually grow angry and start to *dislike* him simply because you feel so horrible. You may even create a few reasons for your sudden repulsion, just to explain what often can't be explained.

It's an awkward situation. When someone is asking for more than you can give, it's normal to feel angry, frustrated, and impatient. And when you're feeling that way, it's so tempting to be rude, dismissive and merciless. You want to escape. You don't want to see his sad, hopeful face. It makes you feel bad about yourself. You—the kindhearted girl who brings home injured animals—may want to choke the life out of a relationship violently. It's hard to believe that love could be replaced by loathing practically overnight. Fortunately, your goodwill toward the poor guy often spontaneously reappears when the deed is done.

Taking the High Road

Obviously, it's a great test of class to rise above so many bad feelings and behave with compassion. Just keep reminding yourself that the poor guy won't be able to understand what he's done to turn you off. His feelings may not have changed, and you were happy he had them awhile ago.

Don't count on him to behave well in the confrontation, either. He'll have trouble showing his feelings about this painful situation. He might choose not to let on that he's been hurt at all, or he might go on the attack and say hurtful things that suggest he's happy to be rid of you. Afterward, Dumpster Boy might ignore you at school, or worse, say hurtful things to others that reach your ears. You can probably

Offload Etiquette

- Treat your boyfriend as kindly as you would want to be treated if he were the one ending things.
- Let him be the first to know it's over. Don't go blabbing to all your girlfriends that you are going to dump him. If he hears it through the grapevine, he'll feel like an idiot.
- Tell him when you're alone, not at a party where people can overhear and he has to pretend it's no big deal.
- Give him as much space as you can. If you know you are going to see him again because you go to the same school, or work part-time at the same place, try to end things so that he has a couple of days to collect himself before he runs into you.
- Don't tell him over the phone or by e-mail if you've been seeing each other for a while. Do it face-to-face, even though it's harder.
- Never ever get your friends to do your dirty work for you. Completely tacky!

understand why it happens. You can't avoid hurting a guy's feelings when you break up with him. You also can't control how he'll deal with those feelings of rejection. It's not pretty, but sometimes a girl's gotta do what a girl's gotta do.

So take the high road. That means being honest and brave enough to tell him flat-out that you want to stop going out with him. It would hurt a lot more if you started to ignore him or flirt with someone new. That is a disrespectful way to treat anyone. Do your best to end your relationships honestly and maturely. At the very least, you'll have the comfort of knowing you're a class act.

Dear John

When you actually tell him that you want to end things, make it short and bittersweet. You can say that things aren't working out for you, but don't list his faults or lay blame. He won't thank you for hearing that you've started to refer to him as "snake tongue" or "the buttless wonder." You don't need to make this guy feel any worse than he already will for losing a great catch like you. Keep it kind and simple. You can say he's a great guy, but you really aren't ready for a serious relationship. And you can say truthfully how much you've enjoyed hanging out with him (think back, girl). It doesn't hurt to add that you're truly sorry.

Most guys will let it go at that and be grateful to avoid the details. Whatever you do, avoid rambling on about your feelings and needs, and do not get dragged into explaining what changed your mind. It probably isn't something you can easily identify anyway, and you will end up digging a hole, climbing in, and burying yourself. Would you want to hear your boyfriend list all the reasons he doesn't want to see *you* anymore? You may think you would, but trust us here. It hurts like hell.

Let us give you a sample Dump Dialogue:

You: Listen, I'm sorry, Devon. I have to tell you that I can't see you anymore.

He: What? I can't believe it. You seemed so into it.

You: I was, for a while. We've really had fun. But lately, I've been feeling we should be apart.

You mean: Into it? Are you kidding? You've been driving me crazy.

He: Was it something I did?

You: Of course not. You're great. This is about me.

You mean: It was everything you did, pal. It's all I can do to sit here and let people think we're together.

He: Is it another guy?

You: No, I just need some space.

He: There must be *something*.

You: Devon, there's no point in getting into the specifics. I just feel I need to be on my own right now.

You mean: I can give you about 50 examples of why I want to dump you. How about that stupid gift you gave me for my birthday? Or that you never came to the door but just honked from the street, so that I had to run out? Or that you'll only read science fiction? Or that you won't even try tofu? Open your mind!

He: I guess that's it, then?

You: Yes. I'm sorry.

You mean: Hallelujah! I'm free! I'm free!

You can see that it pays to edit your thoughts. Be kind, because you will likely get your turn in time and you will thank him for avoiding the hurtful things he might like to say.

And on a final note, once you've done the deed, stick with your decision. You might find yourself missing him once you've had a break and remembering what you liked about him. But resist the urge to call him, even if it's his birthday. You want to do the nice thing. But in this case, not calling *is* the nice thing, because it will give him false hope that you want him back when you really don't. (Remember the lame jokes?) You're just missing that feeling of connection. If you were going out with someone else right now, would you even be giving your poor ex a second thought? Not likely. So let it go. Give the guy a chance to get over you.

chapter twelve

Under the Dump Truck's Wheels

*R*ing. Ring. RING. **RING, DAMN IT! RING!!!** Every single night for the two months you've been going out, your boyfriend has called you. That is, until four nights ago, when the calls suddenly stopped. You've been staring at the phone for four solid evenings and . . . nothing. You've checked it 20 times to make sure the line hasn't been cut. You've had your friends call in to test it. And now you are faced with the obvious. Unless a freak tornado has taken out his home and everyone in it, he's deliberately not picking up the phone to call you.

What a jerk! You suspected something was wrong the last time you saw him. He wasn't meeting your eyes. He didn't hold your hand. And when you walked along the road together, there was space enough between you to drive a big rig right through. Now that you think about it, he's been acting a bit strange for some time now. You must have sensed it on some level, because you asked him a couple of times if something was wrong. Each time he muttered, "Nothing's wrong. Everything is fine."

You allowed yourself to be convinced. "Everything is fine, he said so," you think. "He'd tell me if something is wrong." But then he didn't call. Right away, you knew—everything is *not* fine. In fact, you're being dumped! You hear the *beep-beep-beep* as the dump truck slams into reverse. There's a stench of burning rubber in the air, and tread marks on your face. Yep, that's you under the wheels, all right, flatter than a skunk on the highway. Roadkill.

But how can it be? You asked him straight out and he told you everything was *fine*. You gave him a chance to admit there's a problem. There must be some mistake. Maybe you should call him and give him a chance to explain. Maybe he needed an emergency appendectomy. Or maybe aliens abducted him. You've soon convinced yourself that it might still be okay and taking a deep breath, you pick up the receiver and dial his number. He answers on the first ring (apparently the aliens have returned him to earth):

You *(all perky):* Hi!

He: Oh—hi. *(His voice is totally flat. Your stomach drops. You already know how this little talk is going to end. But ever optimistic, you try again.)*

You: How are you? *(Oh God, you're positively squeaking now. Well, maybe he won't notice.)*

He: Fine.

You: Oh, good. I was just a bit worried about you since I haven't heard from you for a few days. *(HINT, HINT!)*

SILENCE

Uh, are you still there? *(This can't be good.)*

He: I've been busy. *(Busy? Busy with what? Busy with WHOM? I know your whole schedule, buddy boy, you never used to be **busy**.)*

You: Oh? Well, what have you been up to? *(Brightly, now. Don't accuse him of anything. Maybe he really has been busy.)*

He: Stuff. *(Or not.)*

You: Right, so . . . *(mustering up all your nerve)* are we still on for the movie on Saturday? *(Oh please, oh please, oh please . . .)*

He: Well, actually, I think I'll just hang out with the guys. *(Oh God, it's over.)*

You: Oh. *(Don't say too much and maybe he won't notice you've started to cry.)*

He: Yeah. *(The bastard! Just control your voice and get off the phone quickly. You can still keep a little dignity here.)*

You: Well, it sounds like you're busy, so I guess I'd better let you go . . . *(A pause—you are still hoping that he will say, "No, wait! Don't hang up—let's talk.")*

He: Okay, bye. *(Coward.)*

You: Bye. Hey—*(CLICK—He doesn't hear you because he hung up so fast.)*

You put the phone down and burst into tears. This really hurts. There's a physical pain in your chest and you can hardly breathe. Is it possible that you could be having a heart attack at your age? How can this be happening? You *really* like this guy and you thought things were going great. Well, until last weekend, anyway. What did you do wrong? Maybe you shouldn't have tried to help him with his science homework. Maybe you shouldn't have joked about his new haircut. (He didn't laugh when you asked if the barber had used a lawnmower.) Maybe you aren't smart enough, pretty enough, tall enough, or funny enough. If only you were cooler. Maybe he's met someone else. You throw yourself on the bed and sob even harder.

Missing Your Cutoff

When you're driving on the freeway, it's easy to miss the signs for your exit. Later, you'll realize with some surprise that the way was well marked, you just weren't looking hard enough because you were enjoying the speed. The same thing happens in a relationship. When you start noticing these warning signs, there could be an offload in your future:

✳ He only calls at the last minute to ask you out, and he doesn't sound disappointed when you say you're busy.

✳ He isn't very affectionate.

✳ He cares less. Even when he knows you're going through a rough time at school, he doesn't ask how you're doing.

✳ He only calls when he knows you're not at home.

✳ He avoids meeting your eyes.

✳ He doesn't tease you much anymore (and you thought he was finally growing up!).

* He isn't interested in planning very far in advance.
* He starts talking about needing space (and he's not thinking about a career as an astronaut).

Beating Him to the Punch

There's a great advantage in noticing these signs early: it allows you to do a "pre-emptive dump." This means you don't wait and give him a chance to dump you. Instead, with all the grace and dignity at your command, you give him the royal heave-ho, and let it be known in your circles that you did. Only you need to know that you saw the signs first. Yes, you'll still feel your heart cracking a bit, but without the public humiliation, it will mend so much faster. The good news is that guys are so slow about getting around to doing the deed that you'll often be able to salvage some pride with the pre-emptive dump.

Of course, this is really more a self-dump than anything else, but it does allow you to save a little face. Even if you insist on forcing the truth out of him, you will often have to chase the boy and "make it official," either by telling him it's over, or by forcing him to tell you it's over. Either way, feel free to "spin" this a bit and say "we agreed we should split," thereby waving some of the stink away from the Dumpster.

Oh, Grow Up

As we've stressed at other points, your average teenage boy just isn't comfortable with the intimacy and emotion that comes with the package of a steady romance. While girls generally like the thought of being committed to one boy, most boys would rather press a flaming match into their flesh than consider being committed to one girl. This isn't to say that they don't like hanging around with just one girl. Many of them do. It's just that once those rusty wheels start turning and he really thinks about what having a girlfriend means, he panics. Remember, he was put on this earth to compete. If he's "won" your heart, then what's the point of continuing the game? Some perverse logic tells him that he's also lost the freedom to compete elsewhere and spread his seed (at least in theory).

When the fear creeps in, it will change the way he feels about hanging out with you. Instead of relaxing and having a good time, he'll overthink the whole thing, start imagining he's crowded, and check out the nearest exit. He'll become overwhelmed by the need for "space." You'll notice his breathing gets higher and tighter as he grows increasingly claustrophobic. He's got one word running through his head and it's "trapped, trapped, trapped." He's about to bust out, baby.

The Sound of Silence

The breakup of a relationship can beautifully illustrate how the gender gap may be as wide as the Grand Canyon. When guys communicate with other guys, they speak volumes with their silences. A strange sort of shorthand develops between them. Since they prefer not to rely on words, guys develop great skill at merely *alluding* to something without actually saying it. Think about those weird hand signals baseball players shoot into their crotches during their games. It's like a primitive sign language.

Girls, on the other hand, like to use all the words they've taken the trouble to learn and combine them into interesting, informative sentences and dialogues. Needless to say, the gentler sex is far more civilized. We tend to be more open about what we mean. We are capable of saying we're unhappy in a variety of ways, so that our boyfriends don't need to read into our silences. Most of us value clarity enough that we are willing to brave some discomfort just to have it all out in the open. Don't count on the same courtesy from your guy.

Hi Tara,

Sorry I've been out of touch, but I've been totally distracted by the whole Bryan thing. He makes me so MAD. I always figured he'd eventually crack and call me to apologize—at which point I'd get on my high horse and give him the boot. But it's been over a week and he hasn't called! I'm starting to worry that he actually thinks he's dumping me—when I'm obviously the one with the right to dump. It would be just like him to manage to turn things around like that. I'll keep you posted if I hear from him, but I'm starting to doubt that I will.

Meg

The Phaseout

If we may generalize for a moment, guys hate taking the direct approach to breaking up with girls. They don't like to talk about emotional stuff, and breaking up is definitely emotional. They're terrified that if they actually say the words, "I don't want to go out with you anymore," you'll (1) faint, (2) make a scene, or (3) cry. The fear of having to deal with that is greater than their frustration at having to drag things out. So they'll tell you everything is okay to avoid the inevitable discussion of what went wrong.

For this reason, many a girl is left with an empty seat beside her where her boyfriend used to be without quite knowing when he left it. There was certainly no announcement of his departure. He just gradually slipped away, hoping you wouldn't even notice. One day you'll look up and wonder, "Where did Eric go?" All that's left of him is the stuff he lent you that he couldn't sneak out without your catching on. What we have here is a "phaseout." You've been informally sidelined. By the time you clue in, it might seem almost silly to bring it up, because it's clearly old news!

Of course, no girl who senses a phaseout in progress wants to see it for what it is. She will not accept that receding smile as a verdict, and may instead undergo the humiliation of chasing her guy and forcing him to dump her. Until you hear it from the horse's ass, there's still hope, right? You think, "He didn't actually *say* he doesn't want to see me any-more, so maybe I'm imagining things." We are masters at making up excuses for our guys.

A guy is reasonably comfortable living in limbo as he phases his girlfriend out. Unless he desperately wants to pursue someone else, he may be content to wait for months to slide you out of the picture without your noticing. If he's patient and subtle, it can happen. But guys who are just developing their craft are often clumsy, and you'll figure out something's up. It's like his body is still there, but his soul has slipped away. Once a girl is onto this, she can think of nothing else. She wants resolution.

If you find yourself in this situation, you may get so weirded out by his ignoring and avoiding you that you'll trap and interrogate him. Let's be clear about this: If you trap a guy, he'll panic and behave very much like a cornered rat. And there's nothing meaner than a cornered rat. He'll strike out at you, saying hurtful things because he feels *way* out of his emotional safety zone. He doesn't really mean to hurt you. He just wants outta there fast and he's willing to chew his way out if that's what it takes.

Grace under Pressure

So. How do you respond when you hear the *beep-beep-beep* of a dump truck backing up? It's easier than you'd think. Say as little as possible. You may be shocked and you will definitely be hurt. That means you could say some pretty terrible things that will come back to haunt you down the road. Trust us, we've done it. Keep your mouth closed and you will be greatly comforted later by the thought that you appeared calm, cool, and collected.

Whatever you do, don't get drawn into a debate about what happened in your relationship. When he's worked up, his filtering device shuts down and he'll say things that you definitely don't want to hear. Remember when we pointed out the unkind things you might be thinking when you pull the plug on your beau? Well, he'll have similar thoughts running through his mind. He's not seeing you as the charming girl he fell for a while back. Sadly, he sees you as a load of stinky garbage and he wants to drop you off at the hazardous waste site as soon as possible. He'll justify his decision to do so if you make him. Here are some things you might hear:

* "I'm not ready for a commitment right now, and I feel you're trying to push me into one."
* "I've got a lot going on right now, and it just isn't fair to you since I can't spend enough time with you."
* "I really want to date other girls. You're not doing it for me."
* "You've gotten too serious about this. It was supposed to be fun."
* "I want to have sex and you're not ready for that. Someone else will be."

There's not one good answer you could give to any of these statements, so why bother trying? What's the point in arguing with someone who's made his decision that he doesn't want to be romantically involved with you? You'll end up feeling sad and pathetic if you do.

It's tempting to prolong the discussion, however painful, just to keep that guy in front of you so that you can "talk things through." You're worried that when he walks away this time, he'll walk away for good. But the path to dignity is a short one. Get out of there before you start crying in front of him, because that's something you *really* will regret. We girls all know that crying is no big deal—we do it over commercials, for heaven's sake—but to a guy, it's a huge deal.

Do not lower yourself by saying spiteful things. That will make you look bitter, and he'll be convinced he made the right decision. Don't allow your insecurities to spill out, either. Your goal is to show so much class that he'll feel lower than the lowest creature on the planet. You prove this by rising above any attack. If he's mean, throw him a look of surprise and distaste. Then show the extent of your class by explaining that while he has hurt your feelings, you appreciate that he's finally being honest with you. Finish him off by telling him you've had some good times with him, but agree that it must be time to move on. Then move it on out of there. Hold your head high, and walk away quickly before you make the mistake of blurting out what you're really thinking:

Exit Stage Left

Keep it to yourself, sister. Walk away from him with such grace that he will begin to regret his decision. Hold your head high, shoulders back. Remember that he's watching you go and he still likes your butt. Then go home and call up your friends one by one and tell them what happened. Agonize if you must (and you're a girl, so you must).

Your pals will help you regain your perspective, and eventually you will realize that if he doesn't want to see you anymore, there's nothing you could have said or done to change that. You *are* smart, pretty, funny, and tall enough, or he wouldn't have found you attractive in the first place.

Obsession

Sometimes it's tough to regain that perspective when all that's left of your fabulous relationship is a chalk outline on the sidewalk. If you're still wailing the blues weeks or even months afterward, you might want to consider the possibility that you are obsessed.

What could cause an otherwise levelheaded, self-respecting gal like you to make a complete idiot out of yourself over the guy who breaks your heart? Surely, knowing the guy wants nothing more to do with you should be enough to send you running. But for some strange reason, the exact opposite may occur. The more he backs away from you, the more you are drawn to him. It doesn't matter that you had been on the brink of boredom in your relationship. The minute he withdraws, you're all over that boy like an ant on a sticky bun. What's up with that?

Tara,

Well, it's been over a week now and I still haven't heard from Bryan. We've been avoiding each other at school too. The really crazy thing is that even though I wanted nothing more to do with him, I thought he liked me enough to chase after me. But now that he hasn't, of course I've decided I want him back. He was sweet to me most of the time. Maybe I overreacted about that whole condom thing. Maybe it was

You're a Fool For Love If . . .

- You phone his house just to hear him say "hello" and then hang up.
- Your friends get that glazed-over look whenever you mention his name.
- You have a cramp in your hand from writing about him in your diary.
- You won't let your family erase his last phone message. You replay it 10 times a day.
- Your bedside table has become a shrine. You've kept every ticket stub from your dates, e-mails he's sent, and his yearbook photo.
- You send him a "let's be friends" card to let him know that it's all water under the bridge, desperately hoping he'll call.
- You spend an entire afternoon shredding his old sweatshirt so now it looks as if a coyote got hold of it. You keep every shred.

just meant to be a joke and I missed it. Or maybe I should have been
more understanding of his physical needs. Maybe I should call him and
chat about it.
What do you think?
Meg

When it comes to love, everyone likes a challenge. What girl isn't
more intrigued by the one she isn't quite sure she can get than the one
who's calling every night? And when the guy you've got has the audacity
to call it quits, it's a major blow to the ego. How *dare* he lose interest in
you? You want to win his affection back, just to prove you can.

Of course, the guy usually plays his part in all this. If he's been
phasing you out instead of making a clean break, you'll become more
determined to hang on to him. By the time you corner him into ending
things outright, the obsession has taken root and you won't be able to
find the "off" switch and turn your emotions into a platonic friendship.

Some guys may string you along, giving you just enough attention
to keep you interested, but ignoring you just enough to keep you
obsessing. You'll use this time constructively to build him up so much in
your mind that no mortal could ever compete (including him!). He'll be
flattered. Who wouldn't be smug about having a hot babe such as you
pining for him?

But how can he *respect* a girl who's desperate for even a moment
of his time? He knows that he ain't that great, so he's wondering what's
wrong with you for thinking he is. Imagine that you had a boyfriend and
you lost interest. What if he didn't accept his fate and disappear? How
would you start to feel about him? It's a sad quirk of human nature, but
you would likely become resentful because he isn't taking the hint and
getting a life. He's obviously longing for some romantic *ideal* of you and
the longer he acts this way, the more you're revolted by his behavior.

Remember this feeling when you find yourself starting to obsess.
You can't force your ex to change his feelings simply by making it
obvious that you aren't over him. In fact, it's more likely that the reverse
will happen. The crazier you get, the happier he'll be to have escaped
you. Save yourself the degradation. Stop the obsession today and get on
with your recovery. And while you're at it, knock him off that pedestal.

Don't miss out on your next great romance by romanticizing something that is long over. It's better off dead, so take it to the cemetery of lost loves and bury the corpse.

Meg,
Don't do it, don't do it, don't do it. Don't call Bryan up just because he didn't crack first and call you. Deep down you know it's the right thing to do. Don't make the mistake of wanting him back now just because it might look like he dumped you. Who cares who actually did the deed? No one will know for sure. I doubt he's bragging to the guys about you throwing condoms in his face. It makes it sound like you were revolted at the thought of having sex with him. Anyway, let it be. Besides, Ian has plenty of cute single friends—double dating would be a gas. Call me if you find yourself weakening.
Tara

chapter thirteen

Move Along, Girls—There's Nothing to See Here

When you're in the midst of an all-out, no-holds-barred obsession, you never take a moment from your hoping and scheming to reflect on all the times your boyfriend acted like a complete jerk—particularly as your relationship started to slide. Remember all those nights you waited by the phone because he promised to call you and didn't? Remember how he forgot your birthday, broke dates, and gave up complimenting you?

No, of course you don't. You've managed to block all that out. Instead, you focus on the good times. You can remember with startling clarity the first time he held your hand, introduced you as his girlfriend, and told you you're beautiful. Amazing how you can recall every fond and funny thing he ever said to you, yet forget all the times you were embarrassed by his existence.

There is a name for that kind of thinking. It's called "false memory syndrome," and it happens when you imagine your past to be quite different than it really was. If you've been obsessing for any length of time, you have probably built up your relationship with that ex-boyfriend into one of the great romantic tragedies of all time. You're thinking Romeo and Juliet, torn apart by fate, victims of the cruel age we live in. True, he seems to be taking it well. Rumor has it he was kicked out of class last week for having a laughing fit—but he's crying on the inside.

You have conveniently forgotten that you considered breaking it off with him dozens of times. His table manners, for example, almost brought you to tears. Remember how he'd put the entire chicken wing in his mouth and then pop it out, picked clean? Or the way he embarrassed you in class by deliberately giving the wrong answers. He thought he was funny, but he just looked stupid—and that means people thought the best you could do was a goof. But, no, these thoughts have fled, and your mind is filled with images of undying love.

Back to Life, Back to Reality

Give your head a shake, girl! You've given in to a glorious fantasy that would burst like a bubble if you opened your eyes and took a good look around you. Yes, you do need to mourn the loss of your relationship. Go ahead and indulge in a little self-pity. Write about every heartbreaking moment in your diary, play sappy songs, do what the two of you used to do, analyze and overanalyze with the girls. Do it up right. It's kind of fun to abandon yourself to the Drama Queen role. But it's important to give yourself a deadline. Don't let this mourning continue for weeks or months unchecked.

The post-breakup depression is very seductive. Hanging out at Heartbreak Hotel has a definite appeal. It helps you escape the hard work of recovering. Your friends and even your family will indulge you—for a while, at least—and you can just immerse yourself in sorrow. Fortunately, you'll get fed up with living on the dark side and get a taste for sunshine.

For your own sake, do it sooner rather than later. Life is too short to be living in the shadow of a lost love. But no one can wave a magic wand that will get you over him and feeling better. What's required is a conscious decision to do it for yourself. So make the decision, and then:

✳ Call the girls and tell them you're ready to bury that boy and all the bad feelings he brought into your life. Book a date for the "recovery bash" we described earlier. You'll need to collect your photos of him for a good game of darts. But hang on to the ugliest snap you've got, ideally one in which he has a few large zits and very bad hair.

* Next, delete any messages you've been saving. One of us saved a voicemail for many months after an ugly breakup, faithfully resaving it at intervals until she was ready for "the cleansing."

* Take all sentimental keepsakes and start a little fire. Do this very carefully, now, in the fireplace. It's nice to have a sympathetic friend over for this little ritual. She can stand by with the fire extinguisher. Say a few touching words about all he meant to you as you light the match.

* Finally, make a list of the creepiest things he ever did to you. Now make a second list that includes the habits that bugged the crap out of you. Write down a few things that embarrassed you (e.g., mispronouncing words, pretending to know more than he did about a subject). If your memory needs a kick-start, call up your friends. They'll be able to help you out.

Now, whenever you are tempted to call him up, or find yourself plotting how to run into him accidentally, pull out those lists and read them. Then pull out that hideous snap of him and ask yourself: "Is *this* what I'm sad about losing?"

Disappearing Act

Your best bet for dispelling obsession is to avoid him. That's right, you must make an effort to disappear. Okay, you'll have to show up for class if he's in it, but otherwise, scram. For however long it takes—at least a couple of weeks, and more likely a month—you must skip the parties he'll attend and take routes he never strolls. This aspect of your recovery is vital.

And keep busy while you're avoiding him. The goal is to crowd the image of his face out of your brain. Accept every offer to do something with your friends. Take an art class. Volunteer somewhere. Just do something that distracts you from your obsessing about him. It works beautifully. The next time you run into him, your heart may still drop into your boots, but it won't set off the same intense cycle of desperation. After all, there's no time to pine. You've got your sketch class tonight and there's a male model coming in to pose nude. What an excellent distraction!

Friends Forever?

A word to the wise here: Don't waste your time trying to be "friends" with your ex. Yes, there are some fine examples of former lovebirds who made it work, but it's rarely worth the effort. The specter of physical attraction will continue to haunt you both. All romantic relationships are based on a foundation of lust. When you split, this attraction doesn't dry up, leaving you free to do the friends-thing. You wouldn't still be pining for him if you found him revolting, now would you? When there's an undercurrent of attraction between male and female pals, it usually ends up disrupting the harmony.

Besides, it's almost impossible for the rejected person not to continue hoping for reconciliation when the contact is maintained. On the scale of torture, watching someone you still luv start dating other people rates pretty high, even if you're now defining yourselves as "just friends." Why put yourself through it? You've got enough friends and you don't need to keep hanging out with your ex. When enough time has passed, you might be able to spend time with him in a purely platonic way, but you'll need to make sure you are completely over him to do this. Wait until you are happily dating someone else before you even give it a try!

Tara,
I thought about it, and you're right. I guess I just can't stand the thought of anyone else having him. I realize that calling him up to get him back would only delay the inevitable— we would break up again. I just wish things had ended a little better. I am not going to waste any more e-mails moping about that guy. From now on, I'm going to act as if I'm over him so that maybe I'll convince myself that I am.
Meg
P.S. How cute are Ian's single friends? I'm not ready to start dating yet, but I wouldn't mind knowing!

The best way to make yourself feel better about your situation and take your revenge on that guy is to forget about him—or at least try to *appear* as if you have. It's amazing how faking something with energy and conviction can actually make it come true. Pretend you are having fun when you're out with your friends at first, and soon you *will* be having fun. Move on with your life so quickly and thoroughly that he'll wonder if he ever meant anything to you. That's definitely what you want. Nothing will annoy that boy more than losing his number one fan. Let him suck up your dust as you trot off into your own happy sunset.

New Beginnings

Will he ever come back? It does happen, but generally it's *after* you've already moved on emotionally. Many a guy realizes how much he really does love you when he sees that you're living a fabulous life and he's not part of it. When you've become Ms. Independent again and you're not wasting a second pining for him, he thinks, "Man, she looks good. I wonder if I could get her back."

By the time he rediscovers you, you'll truly have moved on, and can't imagine "going backwards"—which is how a relationship with him will feel. Why throw the car into reverse when you can keep on racing forward? Besides, the problems that tore you apart in the first place have rarely disappeared. At least with a new guy, you can have a fresh set of problems, right?

If he doesn't come back to you, trust us when we tell you that your feelings for him *will* fade over time. We know that's difficult to accept—or even believe—at the moment of the breakup, but it's true. As lousy as you may feel right now, one day soon you're going to wake up feeling better in spite of yourself. A week or two later, you'll realize that 24 whole hours have passed and you haven't thought of him once. That day will turn into a week, which will turn into a month, and before you know it, the entire situation will just be a memory hilariously rendered in your Recovery Scrapbook.

And of course, you'll find yourself with a new crush soon enough. You'll be surprised at yourself, since you vowed never to love again. At first you'll feel a bit guilty, as if you're betraying the memory of your lost love. Don't hesitate for a moment though—there's the cliff and over you go! It's all part of the cycle of love.

part three

Parents: It's All Their Fault Anyway

chapter fourteen

You Can't Live With 'Em . . .

*P*arents. Now's there's a topic you were probably hoping we'd forget to mention. But we couldn't neglect to say a few words about those people who brought you into the world and are doing their very best to escort you to adulthood, in spite of your efforts to leave them in the dust. So while you're waiting for that next fabulous boy to come along, let's kill some time by examining your life on the home front. We'll start by taking your family's pulse to make sure everyone is still alive. Please take a moment to answer the following questions:

Let's start with your parents:

* Do they walk around with dazed, stricken looks on their faces?
* Do they startle easily if you fling your bedroom door open with a simple crash?
* Do they refuse to knock on your bedroom door before opening it unless you freak daily?
* Do they snatch the TV remote from you after fewer than 20 channel changes?
* Do they stare at you when they think you're not looking?
* Do they casually listen in on your phone conversations or try to look over your shoulder when you're logged on to see if you're in a chatroom talking to creeps?

And how about you?

* Do you spend most of your time in your bedroom trying to figure out a way to move out?
* Do you say very little unless it's to point out flaws in parenting style, television programming, the school system, your brother's behavior, the weather . . . ?
* Do you announce at least weekly that your parents have ruined your life?
* Do you deliberately withhold information from your parents just to annoy them?
* Do you deliberately provide information just to annoy them?
* Do you refuse to eat the meals they prepare, yet check the fridge hourly and note loudly that you are: (1) starving and (2) appalled at the groceries they buy?

If the answer to five or more of these questions is yes, the truth is pretty obvious. You're a normal teenager and your parents are suffering from growing pains (yours). Our diagnosis: trouble in paradise.

So what's the big deal, anyway? Puberty happens. No one gets to skip the second decade of life just because it's uncomfortable for all concerned. If you feel ready to get on with the business of running your own life, shouldn't your parents step aside and let you do it? Well, maybe they still think it's *theirs* to run. After all, no one sends out a notice to parents when you hit puberty to tell them it's time to ease up on the brake. And so they continue to think of you as *oversized children*, as opposed to the *underexperienced adults* you really are. No wonder there is tension when teens and adults live in a confined space.

We'd like to share a traditional family Recipe for Disaster:

Select one teenager who thinks she's ready to take on the world and combine with one or two (up to three or four) parents who are reluctant to hand over control on demand. Add a pinch of stress and shake vigorously. Pour into a flambé pan, sprinkle with moodiness, and fire up the blowtorch (remember to put on protective eyewear for this). Run for cover. From a safe location, watch your home combust. When the dust settles, start all over.

Here's some background on the problem. The minute you hit puberty, generally around age 13, hormones trigger a lot of interesting changes in your brain and body. The changes inside your head may be less obvious, but they're no less powerful. Somehow the "independence switch" gets flicked on, and your brain begins to issue orders that are at odds with your parents'. Suddenly, you discover you're trapped with maniacs. "Run, don't walk, to the nearest exit," your brain urges. In fact, some days you just want to scream: "Get outta my way or be trampled."

Yet there are your parents standing in your way—leaping into your path, in fact—and seemingly unafraid of being crushed. But there's one thing we want to tell you straight off: They *are* afraid. They are *very* afraid. If you look closely, you will see the twitching of an eyelid or the flaring of nostrils. You'll notice they're haggard, as if they aren't getting much sleep, and they've got that sour, constipated look. That's a good day!

Bad Press

It's hard to believe that they can be so thrown by the simple realization that you're a teenager and that life as they've known it will never be the same again. You'd be surprised how long it can take for them to adjust. In fact, they can continue to consider you their precious, adorable—and cooperative—little girl, even when there is a great deal of evidence to the contrary (including the fact that you are taller than they are).

Why such fear over your looming adulthood? It's because they've heard terrible rumors about teens. You will no doubt have heard some yourself: you're pushy and obnoxious, perhaps, or impulsive and unpredictable. In short, they've heard that you are *dangerous*. Imagine how you'd feel to be told by reliable sources that the devil's spawn has moved into your home?

Let's take a look at these so-called reliable sources. First, your parents' friends and coworkers mislead them with exaggerated stories about their own teenagers. How about those television documentaries on teen violence, teen pregnancy, teen depression, and teen drug use, just to name a few? And let us not forget the rows upon rows of how-to-survive-the-teen-years books on the shelves. God only knows what they're picking up on the Internet!

Perhaps the worst culprit is teen TV. Why on earth do they air shows for teens at a time when any parent could watch? These shows should be scheduled for the hours when most parents are still at work because parents' TV viewing must be carefully supervised. Sometimes you need to talk them through it.

At any rate, there's a lot of misinformation out there giving teens a bad name. It's unfair, but true. Decades of bad press have gotten your parents mighty spooked.

A Visit to the Zoo

Now you have a word for that weird expression you've been seeing on your parents' faces: panic. Some might use another word, *denial.* If you haven't encountered this one before, it's what happens when someone looks into the face of a grizzly bear and calls it a rabbit, because he or she just can't believe it's really a grizzly bear. Not that teens are grizzly bears—this is just a useful analogy. You might growl like a bear, hibernate like a bear, even smell like a bear (there are things you can do about this), but your parents may *still* see a bunny. By this point, they're so deeply confused that that you could chew their legs right off and they'd offer you a carrot.

There's no big secret behind their confusion. They are just seriously rattled by the fact that you are zooming toward adulthood in a frightening world they know way too much—and yet not enough—about. They think life has just gotten too complicated too fast. Only a year or two ago you were their little girl who (mostly) did what they said. Now you have an opinion on everything, and they can see ahead in the not-too-distant future a time when you will truly be making all your own decisions. What's more, they still have to get you there, alive and kicking. They see this as their responsibility. They signed on for the full-meal deal.

You can understand their confusion. You probably have moments when you feel panicky. But as a teen you have the luxury of indulging in panic and confusion. That's what adolescence is for and adults know it.

Parents, on the other hand, are there to offer structure and support to keep you from drifting too far off course and doing permanent damage. They can't afford to panic.

The Book

Keep in mind your parents never got a moment's training. Colleges don't give out parenting degrees, so they just have to fly by the seat of their pants (take a moment to picture this), and rely on the techniques their own parents used back before the dawn of time.

They even use same handbook. We are quite convinced that when we're born, there is a note attached to our big toe explaining to parents where they can find a copy of the book *Parenting in the Dark Ages*. It's been out of print for centuries, but somehow they get hold of it, and it's the source of those annoying things they say:

* "As long as you are living under my roof, you'll live by my rules."
* "Because I said so."
* "If Suzie jumped into the lake/river/ocean/off a cliff, would you?"
* "Wipe that stupid grin off your face."
* "You used to be such a nice girl." (*What am I now? A grizzly?*)
* "Don't use that tone with me, young lady."
* "I suppose you think the world revolves around you?" (*Uh, yeah . . .*)

Once Upon a Time . . .

The Book doesn't even have a chapter on adolescence. Parents in the Dark Ages didn't have to worry much about trouble with teens. By the time a girl was 13 or 14, she was handed over to a nice, respectable, older husband. She was out of her parents' hair before they could even say the word *teenager*. In fact, the word wasn't coined until the 1940s.

At your age, the fun would be over. No raves at the local castle for you. Why not? Because you'd likely have been a parent by your midteens.

If this sounds harsh, consider that during this period, adults generally died by age 40. Treat your folks with a bit more respect, girls. They're already antiques.

Since puberty didn't come any earlier in those days and kids left home by 14, parents didn't get much experience with people at your current stage of life. In fact, adolescence is a fairly modern concept. As a result, parents today don't have the genetic wiring for, or even a long tradition of, dealing with teenagers. It's all quite new.

What we're trying to tell you is that parents today are still pioneers when it comes to having teenage kids around. You will need to cut them a bit of slack because they're figuring out the rules as they go—and they really need your help.

We Are Family

You may be happier already, just realizing how bad it used to be in the modern Stone Age family. Nowadays, there's endless variety in the term *family*.

Maybe you have two parents, one of each gender. That's sort of the traditional model, but there are many variations. You could have a single parent, or two single parents. Maybe one or both of these singles has reattached, expanding the possibilities endlessly for the family Recipe for Disaster described earlier. What if these new partners have a couple of kids themselves, and you throw in your own brothers, sisters, grandparents, aunts, uncles, and cousins?

So, what is a typical family? There's no such thing anymore. The only thing typical is that as a teen, you will think yours is worse than everyone else's. Whatever the structure of your family, it will seem like bad news. We will state for the record that it's easier to manage only two parents. Whether it's one, two, or more, expect that everyone intends to run your life just at the point when you discover you'd like that job yourself.

Is It Hopeless?

By this point you may be feeling a bit discouraged. After all, none of this is your fault. They brought you into the world and biology has simply carried you along with its irresistible force. You're just looking around and wondering, "How did I get here?" But your parents may not answer in a language you understand. Meanwhile, they're waking up in horror every morning knowing there's a dangerous teen in the house. In other words, it's meltdown time. One day soon you'll find them alone in their rooms, rocking back and forth, eyes closed, fingers in ears, chanting a lullaby.

Amazingly, even parents at this advanced stage of deterioration *can* be helped to live full and happy lives again. But it will take work. Are you up for the job? It's time to get on with the business of creating the family you want. It's all about taking charge, girls. Read on!

chapter fifteen

Who's the Boss? (That Would Be You!)

So what can you do about your parents' behavior? More than you've been led to believe, we can tell you that much. Although they've been the boss of you all your life, they do not have all the power—not by a long shot. But let's face it, they're not going to surrender control easily. If there's one thing we can tell you about power, it's that no one likes to lose it. The minute you hit puberty, their power began to diminish ever so slightly. You began to challenge them on every decision because you're on the rocky road to becoming your own person. It's called self-rule, and it is good. It takes awhile to reach this destination though, and that is also good.

Time has a way of sorting out even the most difficult situations, but why wait? As a teenager, you are not supposed to be patient. That's why we're going to walk you through the process of introducing change to your family. Then we'll work on some exercises for training your folks. Your life will improve dramatically, but not overnight. After all, there are still laws that say you can't drive at 13 or take off on your own to find fame and fortune. But you can help speed your parents along the path of accepting your maturity. It just takes persistence and dedication.

That's nothing compared to the work they'll need to do, however. The parenting thing can be rough. The key to what we will teach you is that you need to make it more *rewarding* for them. You need to convince them that allowing you to take control of your life is also good for them. They need to believe that making you happy will also make them happy.

Think like a Boss

It's not enough just to *tell* your parents what you need them to do, although it would be nice if life were so simple. You see, their hearing is already going and they only register about half of what you say. Besides, they're still seeing a bunny—or a grizzly, who knows. At any rate, neither one talks, so you need a different plan of attack.

Let's pretend you suddenly become the boss of a company. Better yet, let's make it the producer of a teen TV show. You choose the show. From now on, whenever we mention "the show," you think about your family. We're going to tell you how to manage your new crew on this TV show. In the process, you will learn about managing your parents and helping them accept your newfound maturity. For the purposes of this exercise, they are your staff. No need to tell them about the game, by the way. That's more information than they need to know—and this exercise is all about providing the right information to the right people at the right time.

Okay, let's set the stage. You are a hot-shot producer known throughout Hollywood as someone who can really turn a show around. You've got the smarts, you've got the discipline and you're heartless when it comes to getting ratings. When they call you in to save *Teen Trauma Drama,* it's in crisis. The audience is tuning out big-time. The director isn't happy, the crew isn't happy, and the "talent" isn't happy. With the decline in ratings, everyone is worried about the future. Who wants to be part of a failing team?

Your mission, if you choose to accept it, is to turn this dud around.

Talk like a Boss

So how do you start off? Do you walk through the door and announce to your new director, crew, and talent (read: your parents) that they're a bunch of losers? Do you say, "I'm the boss, your ratings suck and if you can't turn this baby around, I'll pull the plug and shut you down"?

Well, you could. You run the show, after all. These are "your people." But your people, as it turns out, are already pretty messed up. They heard you were coming and they're terrified. You've got quite a reputation. It's been said that you're unreasonable, demanding, mean, and worst of all, entirely humorless. You can protest that it's all lies but they're already convinced that you're going to fire them.

On the other hand, they knew you long ago, when you were a junior production assistant. You were good at your job and you didn't seem like a heartless ogre then. But power can go to one's head.

They just don't know what to expect and, in the absence of good information, they fill in the blanks with bad information and imagine the worst. They'd like to have a winning show, but any change is upsetting. We humans love to know what to expect when we get up every morning. No surprises, thank you very much.

So that's the state of your staff (read: family) when you arrive. They've realized it's a whole new ballgame and they don't know your rules. What if, just as they've worked themselves into this frenzy, you come in with all guns blazing? What if you start off with a film-diva tantrum? Will this get the reaction you want?

Actually, that approach is more likely to shut down production completely. All their worst fears realized, their performance will slip into a tailspin. They'll be tripping over each other. The shots will be out of focus. Actors will arrive on set without makeup. In short, chaos.

Forbear like a Boss

You may not be quite sure what you want out of this either. It's brand-new territory. You know you want things to change. You don't like the way the show's being run and you want to be the boss. But you also want to do it right. You didn't get to where you are without having some sense.

Where to start? All you've got to work with is this staff. How on earth are you going to turn this sorry bunch into a winning team? It's not as if they are even *trying*, that's obvious. They won't even look at new ways. You overhear them complaining at the water cooler: "But what's going to happen to us now?" "Will we still have jobs?"

(In your family, it will sound more like: "Since when did our lives revolve around her hormones? "Who died and made her queen?" or "If I say it's black, she says it's red; then when her friends say it's black, she agrees.")

This is completely normal behavior for a crew—or a family, by the way—experiencing drastic change. Over time, things will gradually improve even without your help. People can get used to anything. Using the right techniques, however, a good producer and manager can turn things around quickly and effectively.

Work like a Boss

As the boss, you need to stand back and take a good look at the problem and figure out a way to get what you want (which, we assume, is the freedom to make creative choices, run your own show, and find huge success). To do this, you need to be supported by a staff working at peak capacity. You want to be left alone to do your job, but you want them to offer ideas and advice when you ask. Basically, you want them to do a good job (e.g., at parenting), even when there are some changes to the job description. So how do you give them a boot in the right direction?

First, you communicate. Let them know what you want and how their role will change. That's called good direction. It wouldn't kill you to tell these Nervous Nellies that everything is okay, that they're valued employees, and that you have confidence in their ability to do a good job. So what if you have a few doubts? Play nice and tell them you've always liked their show.

Another important aspect of communication is the big sell. You must show them what's in it for them. Advertise the many advantages of the change (Project Adulthood) openly and honestly. (That means you tell them that giving you more independence will reduce their worries, help them sleep better, give them more free time, and ultimately reduce costs. Mention the prospect of romantic weekends alone.)

You'll also need to figure out ways of dealing with negative feelings. ("I've noticed you're in a slump lately, Mom. What do you say we go to the mall together and pick out a new outfit to cheer you up? I'll drive so you can rest.")

And finally, find some change champions. (In a family situation, we're talking about older siblings, aunts, grandparents, even your parents' friends.) These people believe in you and in what you're trying to do. More important, they're trusted and respected by the rest of the crew. Therefore, what your change champions say carries more weight than what you say. A few words from them does more to further your cause than hours of argument and persuasion. Call them and tell them your story. Ask for their help and support. All they have to do is describe a successful experience they've had with you and say, "Give her a chance. She's smart and reliable and ready for the challenge."

Walk like a Boss

The hard part about running your own show is that you have to prove yourself. It's not enough to say the right things, although that's how it begins. You must also "walk your talk" if you are to gain the trust and respect of your employees, which is your goal, by the way. You need to show them that you live by the same rules they do.

Eventually, you have to show you're up for the increased responsibility. If you tell people your judgment is superb, they're going to look for evidence. You must find opportunities to impress them with your common sense and long-term vision. In short, you must deliver the goods.

This isn't as hard as it sounds. If you treat your staff/parents fairly, they will eventually accord you the same respect. They want to see you live up to your commitments. So, if you agree to do something, you need to do it. Simple! No excuses. You say what you are going to do and you do it. Then you do it again, to show it wasn't a fluke. Once they're convinced you're dealing with them in an upfront fashion, they'll be open to letting you do more. You keep coming through and gradually, you make major gains.

And Now for a Commercial Message . . .
Lauren's parents were strict when she was a teen. In fact, they set an embarrassingly early curfew of 11:30. Still, she and her friend Sharon would go out every weekend night, all the

way downtown, because everything fun happened downtown. They were the first to leave every party. At the worst possible moment—usually when the cutest guy came over—Lauren would look at her watch, and say, "I have to go home." She often had to sprint up the street from the bus stop but she always made it on time. The next year her parents not only added two hours, they also lent her the car. She had gained their trust.

If all is going according to plan, your staff should be starting to come around by now. They may even be showing a little enthusiasm, coming up with their own inventive ideas for making things work better. Encourage this and try to use their ideas wherever possible.

You might also consider offering your employees a bonus. Cash is tacky, so why not suggest a staff outing that provides a bonding opportunity? Never forget that your staff (parents) actually enjoy mingling with you. You may prefer the thought of running a needle into your eye, but we strongly advise that you get over it! Really, it's a minor investment of time, yet it has such a generous payoff in terms of building trust. Mind you, don't do it so often that it becomes expected. Even the best employees spoil easily.

Sooner or later your employees will accept the idea that the change is permanent. They will need continued reassurance, feedback, and training for some time, of course, and you must expect some setbacks and minor crises. But their performance will steadily improve as they grow to like being part of a successful show.

It's a beautiful thing—Emmy Award material, really. And it all came about because of your good sense, discipline, and respect for yourself and your employees. You have excellent management skills that will one day take you far.

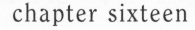

chapter sixteen

Getting What You Want

So now you've learned how to help your parents through the worst of their shock over your transition into young adulthood. Although that's a good thing, there's definitely a downside to it. As they come out of their stupor, they will be a whole lot sharper and you may have to work harder at getting what you want. There's nothing like a tuned-out parent to give into your demands, as you probably discovered by age two. A parent who's paying too much attention is a problem parent. The situation is difficult but not impossible. Remember, you've walked away with the best of their genes. With practice, you can outwit them, but you'll need to present your needs effectively.

They will no longer fall for your requests as easily as they did when you were four and as cute as a button. Now they're so easily put off. A simple swear word—it's just an *adjective*—included in your question can guarantee a "no," regardless of how reasonable the request. A sneer of contempt, though well concealed behind a magazine, dooms your mission. They don't need to see it to know it's there, girlfriends. No offense intended, but when you lose the four-year-old's charm and cop a 15-year-old's attitude, parents become inclined to say no to everything, except for the sarcastic questions. They can usually muster a "yes" for "I guess you'd be happy if I just never left the house again?"

You're going to have to make a few sacrifices to get what you need. Sometimes it will mean biting your tongue. Other times, it will mean saying nice things that may make you gag. No doubt you already realize that there's a price tag attached to almost everything of worth. Sometimes, if you want something badly enough, you have to be *good* to get it. Fortunately there are just as many occasions when it's enough just to be *better* than they are. We're talking about skill, here. It all boils down to developing a strategy for getting what you want and practicing until you get it right.

Who's Got the Power?

Among the many problems that you currently face is the annoying fact that even though you are now quite grown-up, you still need permission from your parents to do anything outside of attending school. That is a drag of considerable magnitude. And so is the fact that you need their help when it comes to financial matters. However, your impression that you have no say in what goes on at home is completely false. Call it your parents' dirty little secret. It's been easier for them to have you believe you have no control, especially over the purse strings.

Pick up any newspaper or magazine and you will see articles describing the huge influence teenagers have on their families, particularly on how their money is spent. In a world where money often equals power, that makes you very powerful indeed. Every big business, from entertainment to the fashion industry to high tech, is courting you. They pay big bucks to market research firms to find out every detail of the likes, dislikes, and spending habits of your generation. The company that best predicts your next big interest has it made.

So how does it feel to be the hottest new target group in a consumer-driven world? To be the trendsetters in the new millennium? Bask in your power. Not only do you spend money on your own "toys," you influence many of your family's purchases. Look around and ask yourself, *Did I suggest this brand? Would they have bought that computer if I hadn't begged for it?* But it doesn't end there. You choose where you eat, what movies you see and what everyone—from Mom to your bratty sister—wears. All you need is parental consent and a debit card and off you go!

It's All in the Training

We realize that you're not just about spending, spending, spending. You also want to be able to do what you want when you want. That's where the folks can be especially troublesome. They so often think they have a say in your plans. Okay, who are we fooling, here . . . They *do* have a say in your plans and they remind you of it every single day. You're happily pushing the pedal to the floor when the screeching of brakes sends you hurtling into the dashboard of life. The folks have come up with another reason to spoil your fun. Use some of your financial clout to buy yourselves an airbag, ladies, because it's going to be a bumpy ride.

So how do you get them to give in on some of life's battles? There are several techniques we'll coach you through, but the overriding advice we can give you is that it's usually best to get them so thoroughly confused that they *think* they've won. Your goal is to leave your parents utterly satisfied, even smug, about their decision to let you do something. This requires convincing them that they are the cleverest, kindest parents on earth, and that their excellent parenting has prepared you for a life of health, happiness, and success.

That means you'll have to be *nice*, but never nice enough to arouse suspicion. It's part of the new training regimen. People are not so very different from dogs in that they benefit from proper training. Do you want them leaping about unchecked and barking frantically, or do you want to be able to take them anywhere, confident in the knowledge that they know how to behave? Well, as any pet owner will tell you, it's as much about training yourself as training the dog. Good owners beget great pets.

Silence Can Be Golden

Let's begin with a word on effective communication. It's the key to all things, girls, and the sooner you master this skill the easier life will be. Knowing when to speak and what to say will stand you in good stead all your lives—in every job, friendship, and relationship—so you might as well start rehearsing with your family.

It's a simple rule, really. *Less is more*. The more you talk, the more trouble you get yourself into. A monologue invites someone inside your head. Think about it, is it pretty in there? It doesn't take much to loosen a tongue, sometimes dead air is enough. We feel compelled to fill a silence. Keep in mind that your words can and will be used against you, especially if the audience is your parents. Nothing is "off the record." They can link a fragment you mumbled six weeks ago to information you babbled today with the speed of the best computer, and you can find yourself in your room taking a time-out before you even realize you spilled the beans.

It's hard to learn when not to speak. Have you ever seen a snake that's swallowed a rat? That's what it feels like to be aching to say something but know you really can't. If you say it, it will backfire and you will not get what you want. So you swallow that cutting remark, or clever retort, and it sits like an undigested rat in your gullet. Take our word for it, sometimes you can express yourself most effectively by not saying a thing.

Key Messages

Parents want you to talk. They will go to great lengths to wrangle a word or two out of you. They worry about what's going on in that mind of yours and whether it's dangerous. When they finally get you going, they're usually relieved—and disgusted—to find that what you're most worried about is what color lip gloss to buy or whether the new guy in school likes you.

It's a complex thing. They want you to say what you think, but they're often appalled when you do. What they want (what they really, really want) is for you to say what they want to hear. Frankly, that goes for most people. Of course, you've been focusing on saying the exact opposite of what your parents want to hear for so long that it will come as a shock that we're proposing an about-face. Start saying some of the things they're just hurting to hear.

It's not as hard as it sounds. You will need to develop a few "key messages" that you can pull out whenever your mother gets that anxious "Is she *really* okay?" look. That's your cue to ramble on for a bit about your day, inserting some key messages. Mix them up a bit, but make sure you cover each one over the course of a few weeks. Here are some good ones to put into rotation, but feel free to develop your own.

1. I like my life, and the person I'm becoming.
2. I like school—or at least I don't hate it—and I realize that education is important.
3. I like to eat. I don't buy into the media hype that thinner is better.
4. I want to be treated with respect just as I treat others with respect.
5. Relationships are important, but the world does not revolve around guys (don't choke).

Oh, we know, these sound horrible. You can't just spit them out like that, or they'll sound contrived. You must use your own words and subtly weave them into a story. For example, you could tell your mother about the kid at school (there's bound to be one) who looks anorexic. You feel so sorry for her, because she's had to quit track since she doesn't have the speed anymore. Your mother's eyes will bulge, as she desperately tries to recall the last time she saw you down a pizza. That's when you hit her with it: you think fitness and healthy eating are the way to go.

We are not by any means suggesting you lie. We definitely want you to believe what you say. These are good things to believe, and if you say them often enough, you'll sound pretty convincing because it will become what you think. Don't keep these positive thoughts to yourself, though. Repeat, repeat, repeat. They're meant for sharing and your parents will not be able to get enough of them. Remember, the better adjusted they think you are, the more inclined they will be to set you loose on the world. They need to know that you respect yourself enough to keep yourself healthy. If they're confident of your self-esteem, they won't worry so much about your safety out there. Think them, say them, repeat them endlessly—and watch how your world turns around.

Your Secret Weapon

It's important to keep in mind that no matter how much you may be pissing them off these days, your parents are still filled with a great (sometimes baffling) fondness for you. Equally important, they are also filled with incredible *guilt*.

It works something like this: Take two normal people, rather like yourself—each sharing half your genes, in fact—and watch them become parents. Goodbye *normal*, ciao *fun*, so long, *cool*. These two people get together and have a child and it's hello, GUILT. They become so awed by their new responsibility that they begin to wonder if they are good enough, strong enough, and smart enough to steer you safely through the dangerous waters of a wicked world. The guilt rolls over them in a monstrous wave. They feel guilt for all the rotten things they've ever done in their lives; guilt for all the worry they caused their parents; guilt over the state of the world today—especially this last point.

As they watch the news at night, you'll see the questions forming in balloons above their heads:

Are we good parents? Is it really tougher being a teenager these days? Is she growing up too soon? Are we teaching her the right things? Will she get skin cancer because our generation burned bigger holes in the ozone layer? Is she eating enough? Are we spending enough time with her?

It's very sad, but ladies, it's also very useful because it gives you a chance to *reward* them. You can help your parents feel better and get what you want, simply by making an effort to relieve their guilt. As any good trainer can tell you, the trick is providing positive reinforcement. Just as you offer a seal a fish after he's bounced a ball off his nose, you must reward your parents when their behavior makes you happy. There are many ways you can toss them a "fish," and no one knows better than you how to put the smile on their whiskery little faces. Maybe you haven't even seen one for a while. They get so caught up in their busy lives, they don't stop to smell the fish often enough.

In fact, there is no better way of rewarding your parents than to relieve their guilt. You will not really diminish their supply by doing this—it is replaced every night with the news of another disaster. But you can give them a few moments of blissful release simply by hinting that you're *happy to be alive*. This is especially important with mothers, who carry the heaviest burden of guilt. Men (surprise, surprise) are often better at finding the "off" button for guilt. So save it for Mom, and pour it on when you see she really needs it. Even when you're not after anything in particular, make her a cup of tea, throw in a load of laundry, and watch that smile appear like magic. She'll think you're a good kid, and believe us, that will help you plenty.

Easy stuff, right? But be careful to be subtle in your use of positive reinforcement. The rewards must be small and frequent. If you suddenly decide to dust and vacuum the whole house in one afternoon, you're asking for disappointment. Nothing sounds the parental alarm bell sooner than a teen who wants to clean. They will know that you are sucking up big-time and that you must want something very, very badly. This knowledge puts the power back in their hands and you will be shot down in flames, baby.

The Direct Approach

Working the parental guilt thing isn't the only way to achieve your heart's desires, of course. There are many devices you can keep in mind while plotting for something that requires your parents' permission and/or resources.

You could, for instance, get a part-time job. Wait! Don't close the book! We haven't lost our minds. There's a method to our madness. Getting a job is obviously an extreme tactic, but think through all of the angles. First, understand that we're not talking about anything too strenuous here, nor are we suggesting that you need to work very often. It's mainly a gesture intended to generate admiration in your parents. Second, consider that you could find a job that is fun and allows you to meet people. The two of us met on the job as teens ourselves. And third, you will earn your own cash to spend on anything you like. Parents know that they lose some power to comment on the purchases you fund yourselves, so you may find your mom keeps her eyebrows where they should be when you walk out in the new short shorts you bought with your first paycheck.

And what about when you're saving for something a bit bigger than a pair of shorts? The beauty of this solution is that your earnings can multiply. Say you set your sights on a cell phone. Clearly, working a few hours at the donut store won't finance it. Explain your goal to your parents, and watch how their attitude changes. They'll note that you're making an effort. They'll evaluate the worth of your goal (a cell phone = accessibility), and they'll likely cough up the extra bucks to ensure your 24 hour availability to your friends in no time. Obviously, some goals will be out of your snack bracket until your jobs become a bit more profitable, but it never hurts to aim high!

There's another surprising benefit to having a job. The folks will be mucho impressed by this move. They'll be so proud of you that you'll probably be granted a few more privileges than you had before. In their eyes, you have become Responsible Girl.

> *My sister took a job at McDonalds the day she turned 16. Now all of a sudden, my parents think she is just so great. They totally spoil her. If she has to miss one dinner for work, they cook her favorite stuff the next night. They couldn't care less when I missed dinner last week because I got home late from the mall. She gets to yak on the phone all the time and she always gets permission to stay out late on the weekends. They say she deserves a break now because she is working so hard. Give me a break—she only works a couple of nights a week and she loves it because she is meeting tons of guys and spends all her money on cool new clothes.*

Enough said about the job scam. As with so many things in life, it's all about perceptions and learning to "spin" something to your advantage. What's spin? It's what happens when someone takes a garbage can, spray-paints it gold, and calls it art. With a convincing enough ad campaign, people begin believing even the wildest story is true.

Timing Is Everything

Another key to getting what you want is getting the timing right. Choosing the right moment to ask can have a dramatic effect on the answer you receive. Basically, the "right" time is when your parent is so distracted that she is not sure of her own name, let alone yours. You seize the moment to slip in your question, which we must add, should look deceptively simple on the surface. Pay attention to the spin, but don't overdo it and risk attracting undue attention with your glossy presentation. Aim for the question that arouses no suspicion and deliver it in a casual tone of voice. If you're nervous, wait until you calm down, because it's a proven fact that the smell of fear can penetrate any disaster your mother may be handling. She will stop dead in her tracks, cast a wary eye in your direction, and say coldly, "We will discuss this later." That's the kiss of death. You'd better spend some time in front of the bathroom mirror perfecting your "blank" expression.

To test how sharp your skills are at phrasing and timing your requests, check out this quiz:

Quiz

Choosing Your Moment

1. "Mom, may I go out for pizza with some friends on the weekend?" (No need to reveal just yet that the pizza joint is actually in the next county and that your friend, who got her driver's license only yesterday after three previous failures and has finally gotten her dad's old beater running, will be the one driving you there.)

   You choose to ask:

   a. When the entire family is having dinner together and your parents are encouraging frank and open discussions

   b. When your father is locked in his woodworking shop

   c. During your mom's meditation session

   d. When your mom is late for work

2. "Dad, could I please have a new five-disc CD player?" (Why would they want you to keep getting up off your butt to change the tunes?)

You choose to ask:

a. During halftime of the football game when your dad's team is losing

b. On a family trip to the store to buy your granny's birthday gift

c. When your folks have dinner guests arriving in 10 minutes and they are still in their sweats tidying up

d. Just after your mom has discovered the pack of smokes your sister keeps hidden in her room

3. **"May I please (courtesy never hurts) go to the amusement park on Saturday with John?" (No need to explain, unless specifically asked, that he is the pierced, tattooed hottie from your local gas station with the attitude they can't stand.)**
   You choose to ask:

   a. As your dad is on his way into the bathroom with the newspaper

   b. When your parents' friends are over for a BBQ and all have consumed a few adult beverages

   c. Right after your single dad's new girlfriend dumps him for a younger guy

   d. When your mom is busy cleaning up dog puke because you thought feeding Fido a jar of pickles would be funny

4. **"Hey, I'm thinking about launching up my own company. Is that okay with you?" (Why bore them with details of your start-up supplies—a bucket and a squeegee—when it's your entrepreneurial attitude they will admire?)**
   You choose to ask:

   a. When your mother is enjoying a bubble bath complete with candles and New Age music

   b. After your dad arrives home from work, describing his boss with words that you would be tossed out of the house for using.

   c. When your newly divorced father is getting ready to leave for his blind date that your crazy aunt Kim set up

   d. While your single mom is apologizing to her new boyfriend because you accidentally broke his new laser disc player

Answers

1. Pizza Paradise

If you answered *a*, *b*, or *c*, we regret to advise that you will not be enjoying any pizzas with your friends this weekend. You will be at home watching educational TV with your parents. Way to go. We're sure your pals will save you a slice. But, if you answered *d*, congratulations!! You are well on your way to a great weekend.

Picture it: It's morning and your mom is very late for work. She is zipping around the place like the Tasmanian Devil, making your little brother's lunch with one hand and pulling up her pantyhose with the other. Her pager and her cell phone are both going off, and it's you, little angel, to the rescue.

While you are pointing out that her sweater is on inside out, why not help her find the car keys, and ask about the pizza thing? Push her aside while she is still making your brother's lunch and take over. (Note: If helping your little brother is too horrible a thought, replace his usual mustard with your dad's hotter-than-hell brand. That ought to soothe your troubled mind.) Why not put together a lunch for your mom, too? (Use the regular mustard.) When you're done, you'll not only be able to go on that pizza outing, your mom may offer to pick up the tab.

2. HiFi Heaven

If *a*, *b*, or *d*, were your best guess, you might as well say good-bye to all thoughts of comfort, because you will still be getting up to get down while your smarter, timing-savvy friends are lounging on their beds letting their remotes do the walking.

Parents in sweats facing the imminent arrival of guests are prime targets. There is nothing more depressing than being found at your worst when your friends arrive looking absolutely gorgeous. Help them out by tidying while they freshen up. Greet the guests and take their coats. Make sure you're serving up those hors d'oeuvres when the folks sashay down the stairs, all gussied up. Stick around and charm the pants off their guests. Getting the bucks for that new CD player will be like taking candy from a baby, babies!

3. The Hot Date

Did you choose *a*, *c*, or *d*? Well, we hate to tell you, but the only kiss you'll be giving ol' Johnny boy will be a kiss good-bye. If you really want that boy, the correct answer is *b*, for BBQ—get it?

Get out there, grab yourself a burger, and work the yard. Tell their friends what great parents you have. Then mention the great guy you've just met. Fill their friends' heads with romantic notions of young love. Later, your parents' friends will have told them the great things you were saying about them, and they'll be feeling quite warm and fuzzy toward you, so . . . ATTACK!!! Hit them with your demands. Make it quick and direct. They'll never see it coming.

4. The Squeegee Biz

If you thought *a*, *b*, or *d* were correct again, we hope that you will enjoy cleaning your parents' cars for the next month because that's how they'll try to "drill some sense" into you. What you meant to pick was choice *c*.

Is there ever a person more vulnerable and insecure than a newly divorced parent about to head out on a date? Now is the time to approach. "So, Dad, I've been thinking . . . You're always telling me to earn my own money and I've decided that you're right." Somewhere inside his distracted mind the words *you're right* will register, because they're words he doesn't hear you say very often. Next, you bring him back to the present, "God! You're not going to wear THAT are you? That sweater is so nerdy."

Then, while he is changing his sweater, say, "I think working will be a growth experience for me." And, before he can become too involved in this conversation, continue with "Jeez, I never noticed how fat your butt looks in those jeans before." As he changes the jeans, flip back to your job chat, "I mean, I won't have to keep coming to you for money." Anything to do with saving money will please him but don't let him get overly interested. "You'd better hurry, Dad." As he's getting into the car, call out, "Have a great time! So are you okay with my job plans?" If he has any strength left, he may try to recall your conversation, *Um, she said I was right, I'd save money . . . What could be bad about that?*

He'll say, "Okay, honey, you have my blessing. Just let me know if you need any help."

Celebrate by calling your mom to let her know that your father is supporting your efforts to become Squeegee Kid.

Tricks of the Trade

We've discussed various strategies for getting what you want, and clearly, it's a cumbersome process. Developing the skills for achieving your heart's desires requires some practice, but we guarantee that the results will be worth it. We'll wrap up by giving you some simple rules that you can memorize and review occasionally. Don't think of these as useful only within your family, either. Many of them will come in handy at school, or with your boss or coworkers at the part-time job you may now be dying to find. They provide an excellent basis for negotiation in almost any situation and will help you keep the upper hand. We urge you not to tackle all the rules at once. Pace yourself. And do remember that no parents are identical.

Be Firm, but Kind

It's easy to make the mistake of being overly harsh and critical with parents. This always backfires when they begin to believe they can never win. If they are convinced that pleasing you is completely impossible, they will soon stop trying.

Don't let this happen in your house. You want them to keep working on becoming the best parents they can possibly be, right? To make this possible, you must carefully manage their expectations. Parents, like pets, are easily discouraged. Although they can survive with minimal attention from you, continual neglect or contempt can permanently stunt their development. They will start to act out to get attention from you in the mistaken belief that any attention is better than none at all. They may start to snap at you and overreact to your minor infractions. They will punish you excessively just to make a point: "I am the parent. I will not be ignored."

You must nip this behavior in the bud. Reward them with fond attention (e.g., "What program would *you* like to watch, Mom?"). Show them your love (e.g., "It would be great if I could meet you for lunch today, Dad."). You could even try giving them an occasional hug. It will surprise and reassure them. What the heck, you could probably use it too!

Conceal Your Disgust

Once in a while, you could sacrifice your habit of walking 10 paces ahead of your mother. We know you do this so that others will assume you are not associated with her—and so does she! Remember that simply walking with her, even if you don't acknowledge her in any other way, is an act of kindness all the more valuable because it's offered in a public setting. This will go far to promote your cause. You can also get good mileage out of simply slapping on a smile. Or perhaps you could open a door for her, instead of walking through and letting it bang in her face. It just doesn't take that much.

Stick to Your Plan

Decide what you're going after and stick to one goal at a time. For example, your goal may be to get your own phone line. List *all* the reasons you will die without one. Strengthen your case by including how the whole family can benefit from the change.

Wear them Down

Be patient. Your parents' attention span is limited, so make your point at 15-minute intervals throughout the day. Speak up at breakfast, call them at the office, remind them at dinner. Repeat. Repeat. Repeat. Keep working at it. By day three, your dad or mom should be able to recite automatically all the advantages of your having that private phone line.

Be Consistent

Focus on one idea if you want your parents to know you mean business. Don't veer off on a tangent about something else or you will confuse them. You *can* teach old dogs new tricks but only one at a time. Keep it simple.

Vary Your Approach

Your parents will catch on to any single strategy you use too often. If one tactic isn't successful, introduce something new. Immediately drop any technique that backfires, but don't consider it a failure. There is no such thing as failure; there are simply opportunities to learn. And remember, the most stubborn parent is probably the one who was best at outwitting his or her own parents.

Knowledge Is Power

Stay in sight, but say as little as possible. The quieter you are, the more likely you will be to pick up information you need. Hiding in your room is counterproductive. Why give them the opportunity to discuss you?

You can learn all kinds of interesting things about your own family just by paying careful attention when they're relaxed and chatty with others. Train your ears to pick up the sound of your parents voices from afar, after you're in bed, for example. You'd be surprised what they come up with, the little schemers.

Keep Your Cool

Never let them see you sweat. If you lose your temper you will lose control of the game. You must be the poster child for "cool."

Teens are masters of "indifference" and this drives parents crazy. They fondly remember a time when you were animated and excitable. Your interest, now so rarely shown, is a huge reward to them. Oddly enough, your anger can be a perverse reward because it's still a change from indifference. They consider your "attitude"—that's a word you'll hear often—a wall they must constantly dash themselves against. They hope to break it down and find the cheery little girl they fear they've lost forever. This is why parents pick fights.

If you're trying to gain the upper hand, you must withhold any reaction. No matter how they joke with you, yell at you, or badger you with questions, do not react. You must be very careful not to let amusement show on your face. Nothing sends an adult into orbit faster than that smirk. You know, the one that says you're toying with them and you find their annoyance highly amusing.

When they finally blow, struggle to maintain your blank expression. If they continue to rant, say in a monotone, "Why don't we have this discussion when you've had time to calm down and think about it? You're obviously emotional and I can't talk to you when you're in that state."

With a move this bold, victory will be yours, even though you may end up enjoying it in solitary confinement!

Make It a Win-Win Situation

You must give to receive, and you must learn to calculate what you can afford to sacrifice for a particular goal. Say, for example, you want to go to a party, but there won't be any adults present to chaperone. Your parents have wisely asked this question directly, leaving you no alternative but to spit out the truth. Do you give it up for lost? Not at all. You offer up something in return. You could agree to be picked up after an embarrassingly short time at the party, or you could agree to take your older sister along, if she'll accept a sizable bribe. Some opportunities are worth the sacrifice. Others are not, and you'll discover soon enough which is which.

Life in the Family Laboratory

Learning how to manage your family will help you develop skills that will come in handy all your life. Think of your home as a lab and your family members as the lab rats. Of course, you'll need to be a little kinder in real-life negotiations, but there's plenty of fun to be had in the practice. Why embarrass yourself in a public setting by using unrefined strategies or by losing control of your emotions? It's far better to rehearse in your home lab. Another day, another explosion in the lab. What the hell—that's what it's there for!

Many of these principles will be useful in dealing with schoolmates, friends, colleagues, and bosses. The last tip is probably the most useful. As much as we may joke, it is important: Do *not* take advantage of the vulnerabilities of others when you're pursuing a goal. Mind you, it doesn't hurt to recognize these vulnerabilities. In fact, that's often how you can turn a situation into a win-win. If you listen and try to understand the other point of view, you'll soon see how you can *both* get what you need.

Other tips also translate well into the real-life setting. It never hurts to plan for what you want and work toward it with patience. Learning to tailor your requests for a particular person and situation will always increase your chances for success. Providing positive reinforcement is something you'll want to do 20 years from now, when you're running your own company and you want your employees to meet your demands.

But the biggest key to getting what you want out of life is *to treat people with diplomacy and respect.* These are the cornerstones of good interpersonal skills. Work out the kinks (and the mean streak) in the "family lab" before taking your skills out into the sunshine. And always leave them thinking that you're the best thing that ever happened to them.

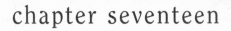

chapter seventeen

Quality Time

*H*ere's a line from the folks that's guaranteed to slam your sphincter shut: "We just don't spend enough quality time together anymore." It's totally normal that you'd prefer to spend time with your friends or boyfriend—or even alone—to spending time with them. They shouldn't take it personally that you find their company boring: they're *parents*. Besides, you live together—how much time with you do they need? It's never enough! There you are, just going about the usual round of your existence—school, work, dates, friends—and all of a sudden you'll hear these words, "You treat this place like it's a hotel." Like that kind of attitude is going to entice you to stay home!

The problem begins with the word "quality." Yes, the definition reads the same in both the parent and teen dictionaries: it means "excellence." But to parents, excellence is properly aged wine or prime beef, while to teens, excellence is something quite different. Teens rarely share their parents' romantic notions of quality family time. Picture if you will, an evening spent around the dinner table, laughing and hugging and maybe singing a few songs in four-part harmony over dessert. To parents, it's a heavenly *Sound of Music* scenario. To you, it's a hostage-taking situation.

Maybe your youthful palate hasn't developed enough to appreciate prime beef yet, and your idea of "quality time" is any time that you spend *away from* your parents. It doesn't have to be this way. You can train your palate to taste the difference quality makes, and a little quality goes a long way. Consider the difference between your basic chocolate bar and a really good chocolate truffle. Generally speaking, a single truffle is far more satisfying than two or even three regular chocolate bars. The same principle applies quite nicely to the concept of spending time with your parents. You will both enjoy it more if the event is short, controlled, and consensual.

Here's an example. Your mother complains that she never sees you, despite the fact that you meet with her twice a week like clockwork to hand over your dirty laundry. She announces that the two of you will spend the evening together. Do you (1) sit down on the couch and watch a full evening of TV with her, or (2) propose going to a movie?

You're tempted to go for the first one because it means you don't have to chat with her during the drive or risk being seen with her. You can just watch a bunch of TV shows back-to-back while she stares at the side of your head and call it a night. It's easy, but it's the wrong answer and here's why: it isn't the truffle hit your mother needs and she'll want at least two more of those plain old chocolate bars.

Choice 2 is the correct answer for several reasons. First, you get points for being seen in public with her. That takes you right into truffle territory. Second, you'll get to see a movie you like, and experience a net savings of at least two hours of your valuable time, because the full movie outing is only a couple of hours. You can afford to throw in a half hour for hot chocolate with the old gal and still be free in record time. If you are actually willing to meet her eyes over your steaming mug and offer an opinion on the movie, she'll go places only chocolate can take a woman and you'll be off the hook for weeks. See how it works?

Back to the Classroom

Hope you didn't think your parent-training sessions were over. Unfortunately it's a job that's never quite done. In this case, we will be teaching your folks that more time with you isn't necessarily better. Right now, they want to spend endless hours in your company. What's more, they think it's their right and their duty to do so, especially now, when you are pulling away from them. It makes them a little overeager.

You can change this. Once again, it's a matter of helping your parents realize what's good for them. In this case, they need to learn that less time with you is fine, as long as it's "prime beef" quality time. But first, you must teach them that when they force you to spend time with them it is not prime beef they're getting, but an all-beef wiener. This complete, you can introduce them to more sensible notions of quality and prove that small amounts of a good thing are the way to go.

If you're an average teen, you've probably hit rock bottom with the folks by the time you're 14. You've learned to sap all joy from your parents' hours with you simply by withholding all attention from them. It pains them that you are withdrawing from them. They fondly remember a time when you were *alive* in their presence. They *loved* that. They *miss* that. They *need* that. And perhaps, as a Diva of Indifference, you taunt them. Does any of this sound familiar?

1. You slouch, cross your arms over your chest, and let your body language scream that you are not susceptible to any of their stupid ideas.
2. You give them the blank stare, the one that you use in algebra.
3. You roll your eyeballs so hard and so often you risk damage.
4. You speak in a monotone.
5. You look at them occasionally with a confused expression as if to suggest they are speaking an entirely different language.
6. You look extra sullen whenever they brag about you (your good marks, musical genius, etc.) to prove that you don't have the personality to go along with this remarkable talent.

If this sounds like you, your parents already know all about "wiener time," and you've done enough. In fact, it's time to begin the retreat. Remember that providing them with absolutely no feedback or information means that they will be forced to imagine what's going on in your mind. They will become overly suspicious and invent ridiculous scenarios. Try this on for size: You went to the movies last night with some dude you've had a crush on for ages, but you do not explain that the evening was a disaster. You caught your date flirting with She-Who-Sells-Popcorn and you are crushed. Trust us, this reality is all over your face, no matter what you haven't said. Your mom asks, "How did your date at the movies go?" You reply, "It was fine." Now worried, what she thinks is, "Oh. My. God. She had sex with him and she's distraught that he hasn't called her today!" Get ready for the "sex talk." Enjoy, loser.

Do you see where we are going here? Too much mystery is a bad thing. Life will go along much better if you let them know that you are more or less okay.

Weaning Your Parents

Of course, you can stall for time with a little technique called "evasion." This means that you must have an excuse at the ready each and every time they ask you to join them on a lame outing. Clearly, planning is of the essence. Be aware that they will try to spring things on you and you must never look panicked or shifty-eyed. Why would you? We are not suggesting you ever lie to your parents about what you are doing or where you are going. We are simply recommending that you always have real plans to do something that will pass the test of parental "worth."

You must never let them feel snubbed, however. No matter how unappealing their suggestion, you must protect their pride. They are offering you a *gift*–the opportunity to spend time together. While it may sound to you like an offer to spend half the afternoon at the building supply store helping your father choose two-by-fours for his latest wood-working project, it is a gift. Why? Because time is not something the parents of teens have in abundance and they consider it valuable. If they want to spend what little they have with you, it's a compliment. So don't just toss it into the mud and kick it around. That's harsh. Besides, hell hath no fury like a parent scorned. All it would get you is more time at home bonding with them than you could bear.

As you wean your parents from your company, they will be highly sensitive to insult and will scrutinize your evasions very closely. As a result, you must always provide the *superior* excuse. You will rarely be able to get away with the "I just want to hang with Maddy" excuse. They will be hurt that you prefer Maddy's company to theirs, especially when they only have a few hours free.

Homework, of course, is the best excuse, and it will pretty much cover any weekday offer of a "quality time" excursion. "Oh I can't, Dad. You wouldn't believe how much math homework I have. I live in constant fear of becoming one of those statistics. You know, how many girls give up on maths and sciences. I'm working extra hard to keep up my confidence." Get on the computer and he won't have a clue whether you're doing some advanced calculations or drifting in cyberspace, but he'll be proud his girly is technosavvy.

They're not impressed by your idea of time well spent. You consider it a productive afternoon if you've spent three hours talking about your latest crush with a friend. It's a bonus if you actually got some shopping or homework done. Therefore, your goal (to remain unstructured) clashes with theirs (to get the most out of every waking hour). Not only will they try to structure your time, they will also factor their company into it if you aren't quick on your feet.

Giving 'Em the Slip

What if you are suddenly confronted by a shockingly lame offer? Are you prepared to slap a refusal on the table with a confident smile? No stammering, "I'll get back to you on that," or you'll be strapped into your car seat before you can even scream, "Don't make me go!" It's gotta be quick, it's gotta be tactful, and it's gotta be foolproof.

The Offer. "Honey, I could really use your help at the office this afternoon. I have 200 reports to collate manually and bind. I'll order a pizza for lunch. It'll be fun!"

Please! What's fun about spending Saturday in an empty office with your mother? We can tell you all about slave labor, because our parents forced us into pricing groceries, stocking shelves, typing reports, filing, you name it. It was grim, babies. There is nothing fun about broken nails and paper cuts. But that's what will happen if you don't brush up on your talent for evasion.

The Slip. "Gee, Mom, I wish I could. That does sound like fun. Unfortunately I've already committed to working at the drop-in center this afternoon. I'll see you at dinner, though."

Girlfriend and boyfriend excuses will never cut it. You'll have to be endlessly inventive in using school-related activities. Weekend sports or courses are excellent excuses, but don't be surprised to find your folks coming along to celebrate your success on the hockey rink or the dance floor. Of course, there's the job excuse as a fallback, but they will always know your schedule better than you do. You're after spontaneity here.

What else can you pull out of your hat? Well, sit down, girls, this is going to come as a shock. We propose that you take up some volunteer work. Don't worry, we aren't losing our minds. Not at all. Benefit humankind? Sure, as long as you benefit yourselves at the same time. No doubt your parents and your school have fed you the line about beefing up your resume with some service to society. That's all well and good. We're just saying that there can be no more worthy excuse in the eyes of a parent than volunteering. If you choose an activity you actually enjoy, you will be delighted to do it instead of collating with your mom.

You'll want to find something pretty flexible. How about walking the dogs at your local pound? You can do that anytime. There's the drop-in center for troubled youths. (No, you're *not* troubled, despite what your parents say and you *can* offer advice to others your age). Maybe you could teach a kid to read or coach a sport you love. There are lots of opportunities that your school can point out to you.

Sure it's a little self-serving, but the best things in life can improve you without pain. Yes, you will benefit humanity. Yes, you will do good deeds and build up a fabulous resume. Yes, you will meet new and interesting people, many of whom will be teens also escaping their parents on a Saturday afternoon. But most importantly, you will be seen as Caring Girl, the one who gives of her time so generously.

Introducing Truffle Time

Now that you've become so accomplished at giving your folks the slip, you won't mind spending time with them nearly as much. No, you're never going to love trailing after your dad in Hardware Heaven. But what if you come to him first and make an offer that is downright bearable? Frankly, he'll be so starved for a moment of Caring Girl's time that you could propose running a father-daughter marathon and he'd be high-fiving you. So how about asking dad on a special outing, maybe a dinner one-to-one. Use this opportunity to deliver some of those key messages we talked about earlier. Let him know in a few simple sentences that you are fine and growing up quite nicely.

Expanding Your Horizons

There's no need to limit your quality time segments to meals. Those parents of yours could be useful escorts to a variety of events. The movie thing gets old pretty fast, so why not consider something more daring—the art gallery or the museum? We know, it's a scary thought, but chances are you won't meet anyone you know.

Be prepared for your parents to put up a bit of a fight here. You know how caught up in the rat race they are. An afternoon at the museum is time that could be spent picking up after Fido in the backyard or making a stew to last the week. Besides, they might be a little intimidated by the prospect of a cultural excursion. That's quite common—maybe you are too. But you never know, you might actually like it.

The special exhibit is the way to go. You say, "Mom, can we spend an hour at the photography exhibit at the art gallery this weekend?" How scary is that? No one is going to come up and quiz you afterward. Maybe you'll even feel comfortable enough to check out the Monet paintings later.

You could try out the museum on your dad. He's always on about some boring historical event, so why not get him to put his money where his mouth is and take you to the museum? While you're there, check out the dinosaur exhibit and make a few fossil jokes to your dad. He'll love it.

So what's the point in making this effort when you could be down at the multiplex checking out the latest disaster movie? You could come out of there with a story to tell your friends or the guy you most want to impress. It may only be a story of how your mother let loose a blood-curdling scream at the special spider exhibit ("I thought they only had *dead* things in here!"), but it's a story you wouldn't have had if you'd spent the day on your arse in a dark theater.

If you're like us, you may sometimes wish you had more to say when you're with other people—stories that are informative or funny and interesting. Well, movies only take you so far, and as conversation goes, you're only as good as the material you get. Interesting people aren't "born that way." They become interesting by opening their minds to many things and soaking them up like a sponge.

None of this means you need to become an expert at anything. We repeat: there is no test. It just means absorbing, understanding, and storing information for future consideration. No one expects—or wants—to hear you spout on about the technique and motivation of some artist during his "mad" period. It's enough to go and look at his work and think about whether you like it. It's *always* enough, with art, music or literature, just to form your own opinion. But you might find, as time goes on, that you become more confident and interested in exploring the "whys."

Time spent on developing yourself, however you do it, is true "quality time." It can be sports, or dance, or reading, or drawing. As long as it makes you feel great, it's making you a more confident, interesting person. That isn't to say time spent just hanging with your pals isn't quality time. It is, but it's good to stretch a little now and then. You can expand your horizons by checking out new things. Just open up your head and let some ideas poor in. You'll be surprised by the connections potent teenage gray matter can make with some new material. It may be 10 years before you find yourself thinking about that painting again, but your memory of it will still be there, stored on your hard drive.

Most of us are sure we don't know enough and we can be a bit shy about sharing our opinions. Who wants to be one of those overconfident blabbers who thinks she knows more than she does? That's how you can really get something out of "quality time" with your parents. You can gain confidence by exploring new ideas and maybe even discussing them. There are some mean people out there who will make fun of your lack of knowledge, but parents are not among them.

Your parents will want to support you to try new things, but they may need you to hold their hand (not literally!) as you head out with them on these adventures. You can become better informed and more confident together. Your mother might have a new story to tell her friends on Monday, too. If nothing else, these outings help your parents relax. And remember, when they relax, *your* life gets easier.

Hit the Dusty Trail

What if your parents lie down and play dead when you mention modern art? Or maybe you just aren't Culture Girl. How about spending that quality time outdoors, taking the rough-and-ready excursion? Maybe they'll take you whale watching, white-water rafting, hiking, or camping. Incidentally, you can meet some cute guys doing these things.

When Hannah was a teenager, her parents hauled her off on many long trips, driving across continents with a trailer in tow. That car felt mighty crowded at times, with the three of them and a really big German Shepherd. Hannah missed her friends and she sometimes wished she could just beam her parents off to a distant galaxy, but there were some highlights. She had fallen in love with hiking as a child and she continued to love it. When she got to college, Hannah chose to study geology, and it became a satisfying career.

Who knows where family quality time can lead? You can turn it to your advantage by finding activities you enjoy and learning all about them. There may be a job in "them thar hills" or you may just find a hobby that brings enjoyment to your life. Taking pictures with your father's old camera on family trips may just lead you onto the camera crew of feature films, as it has one of us. Look hard enough, girls, and there's always something in it for you.

To Like or Not to Like

Here's a news flash: You won't always like your parents, however much you may love them (and you know you do). Do you like everyone you meet? Do you like your friends every moment of their lives? They're just people, after all. We are all changeable creatures, and some of our moods are more appealing than others. Don't expect to like your family all the time.

The world as you know it does not end because you find your dad unlikable some days. Say he actually pursues another driver just because the guy cut him off with his fancy sports car. They have a yelling match on the roadside, complete with menacing gestures. It's close enough to your school that some of your friends witness it. Do they think less of you? No. Amazingly, they don't even think less of your father for very long. He's nice to them and he's never raised a finger to you, so they don't dwell on it.

When you are a teenager, it can be difficult to separate yourselves mentally and emotionally from your parents. Somehow you feel that you are an extension of them and are always measured against them. On some level, you know you love them, but you also know that you often don't like them—and that creates quite a conflict in your mind. It takes many years before you can shrug in the face of parental misbehavior and say to yourself, "Well, Dad is his own person and he makes mistakes. It doesn't reflect on who I am."

You are no doubt already starting to see people as individuals complete with many faults and virtues. In the coming years, you will learn to ask questions and consider behavior carefully so that you can draw a picture of a whole person. You will start to recognize that people have their own agendas that affect whether they like or dislike your parents—or you. And you will see that sometimes personalities clash and there can be no common ground, no liking, no respect. That even happens within families, but not very often. You will likely share many of your family's views, values, and interests and will end up quite willing to defend them against the world.

Generally speaking, no one remembers your parents' embarrassing behavior nearly as well or as long as you do. What stands out in your memory as a grim moment of humiliation barely causes a ripple in other people's lives. Look at your friends' parents: Aren't they complete fools sometimes? Do you review their shameful exploits regularly and think to yourself, "Wow, Mimi has *loser* parents. I guess that means she is full of loser genes too?" Of course you don't! You kind of enjoy that Mimi's mother likes to put a tea cosy on her head and clown around the kitchen as she's brewing tea. But Mimi is turning 18 shades of red and hustling you into the next room.

See what we mean? We are far more indulgent of other people's oddities than we are of our parents'. In your mind, no one is ever as bad as your mom or dad. But no one else is nearly as critical of them as you are. People get caught up in their own fascinating lives and don't think about yours nearly as much as you imagine.

Here's something to keep in mind. If your parents have been embarrassing you more than usual, review your recent conduct. Have you, perhaps, been a little more neglectful than usual? Did you duck and flinch when your mother tried to kiss you last week? Have you lifted a finger around the house? Have they used the words *sass, bold, impertinent,* or *rude* lately? If so, it sounds as if you've been a little stingy with those rewards we've told you about. Go out right now and do something extra nice without asking for a thing in return.

When All Else Fails

There remains one final, startling option for quality time: You could really listen to them. Oh, you don't have to take in every word, but you might just be surprised at what they have to say when they're in the right mood. We realize this advice comes as a great shock and disappointment to you, but bear with us.

The best time to explore this possibility is when you are giving them the truffle outing—the small, but potent quality-time segment. Everyone will be in good spirits. They'll be happy because you invited them out and you'll be stoked because you controlled the situation. Take them right away from their home environment. The dinner out never loses its charms, so use that one when you can. When you are staring across a large pizza at them, let your imagination do some tricks. Pretend, just for an hour, that these are two people who happened to end up at your table. They're generous strangers who will be footing the bill for your dinner.

Practice your conversational skills, which will be so useful in other situations, by interviewing them. Most people love to talk about their lives, and your parents are no exception here. Ask them how they met. Ask them how their parents met. These could be great love stories. What goals did they have when they were your age? How did they arrive at their career choice? Have they enjoyed their work? What did they do that annoyed their parents when they lived at home? Once they've warmed up to the interview, ease your way into the incriminating stuff. Did they ever get drunk when they were in high school? Did they ever experiment with drugs? Did they ever sneak out of the house to go to a party they weren't supposed to go to? You might be able to use some of this ammo against them later!

Remember, their history is your history and it's important to know where you come from when you're trying to figure out where you are going. Sharing history is a powerful human tradition passed along throughout the ages. You may not feel it's anything special now, but there will come a time when you will be glad you know about the people who came before you. As for the people who are with you now, you're stuck with them, and for the most part, that's a good thing. Your parents, brothers, or sisters share a strong bond with you. No one else will ever be able to understand exactly what it was like for you growing up. They know because they are living their lives alongside you, sharing experiences that are shaping the person you'll become. All the day-to-day detail of your lives binds you together in ways you can't fully understand.

You've probably seen evidence of this bond already. What happens if someone says something mean about your brother? You probably feel a rush of anger that surprises you with its intensity, given that you claim to despise him. What if your dad makes strange noises while he chews and your mother sighs every two minutes? It's damn funny if you and your brother are discussing it, but let an "outsider" criticize and the lioness comes out in you. That's instinct kicking in. You can't explain why, but you must protect your family bond. Not even your closest friends can break it.

It's the "blood is thicker than water" thing. All through your life you will do more and forgive more for a family member than you ever will for a friend. It's just the way it works. Equally important, you know that you can count of them in times of trouble in ways you'd never count on a friend. There are thousands of years of genetics behind this behavior, so who are we to question? And isn't it great to know that there are people who will stand by you in the worst of times?

You're also in for a shock one day in the not-too-distant future. You will find yourself doing something exactly the same way your parent does. Maybe you'll glimpse yourself in a store window as you run for the bus and you'll see your mother's distinctive giraffe-like gait. Or maybe you'll see your father's furrowed brow as you scowl at the mirror. When this happens, you will hear in your head a long high pitched scream: "Oh god! I've become them!"

And it will be true. That's the circle of life in all it's glory.

chapter eighteen

Love and the Single Parent

Once upon a time in a land far far away from the countryside and all its inconveniences, there lived a smart, beautiful, and very hip princess named Cindy Ella. She lived in a stylish loft in the center of town with her annoying sister and her mom and dad. Cindy Ella had a bedroom of her own, with a computer in it and a wardrobe full of cool clothes. Even though her parents drove her crazy, Cindy Ella loved her family dearly. She slept soundly at night, knowing that everything in her life would be comfortably the same in the morning.

Then, one fateful day, she returned home from her grandmother's cottage to find her parents waiting for her. "We have some bad news, Goldie Locks," they said, using their nickname for Cindy Ella, who had beautiful, naturally blond hair. Then they told their beloved daughters that they were splitting up. "For a long time now, our marriage has been either too hot or too cold," they said. "It's not <u>just right</u> anymore and we can't continue to live like this." And although the girls huffed and puffed, their parents blew their happy little kingdom down . . .

Would every one of you whose parents are still together, please take a moment to count your blessings? It means that you will have one less thing to agonize over during your teen years: your parents won't be dating. Take our word for it, this dating business becomes ugly pretty fast when parents are involved. Imagine your mother simply holding hands with someone who's a stranger to you. Kick it up a few notches and imagine bumping into this guy coming out of your mother's bedroom early one morning, wearing her flowered bathrobe. First there's the awkward chat over breakfast, then he starts dropping by for dinner, and finally, it's assumed that the guy will stay the entire weekend. Does your mother *care* whether you like him? You bet she does! Will your dislike influence her plans to sign him on permanently? Probably not.

It's seriously annoying, but parents all too often put their romantic needs before the short-term happiness of their kids. They think it's in everyone's best interest to become a new, "reconstituted," happy family. Well, can you really blame them? Will you promise to stand by their sides in sickness and in health from this day forward? Or will you be off to explore brave new worlds on your own in a few years? Maybe your mother would like to roll over in the morning and see someone who's dedicated to her welfare on a permanent basis.

You may not like the people your parents date. And if the new love comes complete with a family all his or her own, that's more bad news than any teen needs to hear. The worst thing is that you won't have a lot of control over any of this.

Smashed to Bits

To say living through the breakup of your parents' marriage is tough is a gross understatement. In fact, it's like someone snatches up the pieces of your familiar world and throws them into a blender. Process at high speed for three minutes, and you get a new, puréed life handed back to you. For a while (and it's usually a long while), all comfort and security vanish. Where's that boring predictability you used to complain about? Where's the order? And where's your other parent? Oh yeah, you get to live in two houses now. That's just what you need, double the trouble: two bedrooms to clean, two sets of rules, and two solo parents who are trying so hard that they're functioning with the ferocity of four. What a picnic!

To add to the good times, your parents are feeling just as confused by these changes as you are. They think it's their fault the house of cards came crashing down. Suddenly the people in your life who are normally strong and in control become unsure. After many years, they're suddenly facing the world alone and this time, they're facing it with the added responsibility of kids. This is one of those uncomfortable times when you will be forced to see your mom and dad as people with the same hopes and fears that you have.

Being forced to deal with such heavy stuff this early in your life really sucks, and we feel for those of you who are currently undergoing a family split. You may think that all your problems would be solved if your parents just got back together, but this is probably not the case. The best thing you can do right now is work toward accepting the reality of a lousy situation. You can make yourself crazy trying to change something you have no control over. Try not to waste good energy wondering where to lay blame or wishing that things were different, because you're not the one with the power to effect change. And it's not your fault, either. We know that you know this, but we have to say it anyway. You are *not* responsible for what happens in your parents' relationship. It doesn't matter how evil you've been lately: **IT IS NOT YOUR FAULT.**

Relationships of every kind—with your girlfriends, with boys, with your family—are tricky. Whenever there's more than one person in the equation, it's a situation beyond your full control. You can't rule how they develop or when they end. Every relationship takes on a life of its own, and the relationship that you have with your parents as a couple is no exception. The more people involved, the more unpredictable it gets. This unpredictability is exciting in friendships or romantic relationships, but not in family relationships.

It's worth mentioning that the ending of a relationship isn't necessarily a death. Sometimes, especially when there were two unhappy parents involved, a wonderful rebirth follows. Is it easy? Ask your mom about birthin': it's a hideously painful experience with a fabulous reward at the end. In this case, you'll witness the rebirth of your relationships with your parents, and if everyone tries hard, there could be great things ahead. Sure it will be different, but different isn't always bad. You may get to know your parents individually in ways you never did before and find yourself growing even closer to them.

Sometimes, no matter how hard people try, relationships end. You can't let this possibility discourage you from developing new ones, because these connections make life worthwhile. You may even find yourself in a fantastic relationship with a new stepparent. Hard to imagine, but it happens more often than you'd think. Keep in mind that you have a role to play in creating the relationships in your lives. They don't "just happen." What you put into a relationship is usually returned in spades. So consider your contribution carefully!

And Life Goes On

However devastated they are at the time of separation, most parents will eventually decide to move on with their lives and this means scoping out a new partner. Dating isn't a breeze at any age, especially not for newly divorced people whose previous experiences likely featured disco. Here you are, in need of counsel on matters of the heart, and there they are, gearing up for another round. Suddenly their advice isn't trustworthy, because they're struggling with the rules of dating themselves. Worse, you could find yourself coaching *them* on the finer points of "getting it on" in the new millennium. Well, it won't be the first time we've suggested coping through role reversal, and it probably won't be the last!

Let's take a moment to consider what's happening to newly divorced parents. Basically, they've been gathering dust for years and making very little use of their hormones. All of a sudden, nature calls again. It's an *awakening*. Substances that were long dormant kick in and transform the parent into someone you may not even recognize. What happens next is frightening for all involved. It's like slamming a car into reverse and gunning it down a dark, twisty mountain highway. We call it the Descent into Darkness, and at the bottom of the hill is the scary land of Born-Again Teenagers. You are on the very same highway, gearing up for the ride of your lives, when your parents go squealing by, totally out of control—truly "accidents waiting to happen." They're in big trouble, because their bodies are no longer strong enough to withstand the rigors of the hormonal rush. They're breaking apart! Only the systems of first-time teens are set up to run on crude, unrefined hormones. Your parents' delicate systems run best on high-test, so when the murky sludge of hormones starts pumping into their bloodstream, bodies soon start colliding with reckless abandon.

So how will you know if the vacant-eyed adult in your home is a Born-Again Teen? There are many early warning signs:

* Your dad trades in his old glasses for turquoise contact lenses.
* Your mom, who has worn her long brown hair the same way for centuries, comes home one day sporting a short, spiky blond "do" and a tattoo.
* Your mother coos over some stupid flower she got on a date as if it has the symbolic value of a rose in a Shakespearean sonnet.
* Your father, who drives his car everywhere (even to the mailbox), begins getting up early to go jogging.
* Either parent asks, "Do I look fat in this?" more than once a day.
* Your mother starts asking you, "Do you think he'll call?" And when he does, she uses "the voice"—you know, the one we all use when "he" calls. It has a musical quality to it and is frequently accompanied by giggling and the words, "Oh, stop it."

Chances are they're just fumbling in the dark and are petrified about the whole thing. Under the influence of hormones, they may put on a good show, but take our word for it, they're worried the equipment doesn't work after years of disuse. You can feel for them, but don't let them turn you into the friend and confidante. Never forget that a mother is a mother is a mother, not a gal pal. Sure, you can offer support: "I'm sure he'll call, Mom," or the ever popular, "Well, it's his loss if he doesn't." After all, this is a stage of exquisitely painful vulnerability in anyone's life, whether it's the first go-round or the second coming.

Sabotage

Both your parents and their dates are going to be desperate for your approval, that's a given. If you accept the new love, their lives will be much easier. In other words, you have the power to make this situation hellish for all concerned. Many a teen has used parental insecurity to disastrous advantage. All it takes is a few well timed comments to set everyone off.

You could, for example, study their courtship behavior closely and look for discrepancies between the way they want you to act and the way they are acting themselves. If your mom's been busting your chops lately over the amount of makeup you wear perhaps she'd appreciate knowing, as she heads out on her first date in years, that she hasn't exactly conquered the natural look herself. "Are those eyelashes, Mom, or spiders nesting in your eye sockets?" And didn't your dad forbid you to go out with that older guy? "Older boys only have one thing on their minds," he said. Make sure you ask him what will be on his mind tonight as he goes inline skating with the 25-year-old he's dating.

Better yet, you could quiz their dates when you meet them:

* Ask about previous marriages and number of boyfriends or girlfriends.
* Ask about convictions or incarceration.
* Ask a guy how much he can bench press, then note that your father surpasses that amount by far (lying in his recliner).
* Ask a guy how tall he is, then say, "Men always lie about their height."
* Ask a gal how much she weighs, then note, "Women always lie about their weight."

Or how about bringing a parent to the brink of despair by the process of "breaking in" his or her new sweetheart.

* You could refuse to meet his date's eyes and deliberately use the wrong name ("Oh, sorry. Karen was the blonde . . .").
* When your dad's new gal calls, tell her that he's at his "group" and allow her to guess that it might be a New Age "men running with wolves" sort of thing. Let him explain his weird life.
* If your mom's out getting a body wax when her new guy calls, be honest. Is it your fault she's hairy?
* When the new gal cooks, gag ever so slightly and comment, "My mom doesn't make it like this."

* Whenever the new guy walks into the room, make a point of ending conversation so that he will think he was the subject of it. When he leaves the room, *laugh*.
* Roll your eyes at everything the new gal says as if it's the most bizarre thing you've ever heard.

Not that we need to give you any ideas . . . We know how creative teens can be in these situations. There's no question that these exploits will bring a moment of evil satisfaction, but they won't make you feel good for long. After all, your parents will be miserable enough about the situation even without your "help." You might be surprised to find you even feel a little cheap after shooting down the new sweetheart's efforts to win you over.

But if it's not your parents' fault, not your fault, and not even the new date's fault, who the heck is going to pay for all this suffering? Everyone. It's a package deal. The sooner you accept that, the easier the transition to your new life will be. This doesn't mean you need to swallow all your anger and resentment—that isn't even healthy and it won't fool anyone. Do your best to tell people honestly how you are feeling, and confide in another family member or friend if you just can't speak to your parents. And do not give in to the urge to be so thoroughly unlikable that the new people in your parents' lives run screaming from the house. This may ultimately leave you disliking yourself, and that's no good!

Besides, being a little more agreeable can have certain advantages in these situations. Read on!

Shiny and New

When they are brand-new with the plastic wrapping still on them, most relationships transport people out of their ordinary lives and straight onto Luv Land. Here, things take on a special glow and there are unwritten rules that everyone follows:

* No one wears torn underwear or socks with holes in them.
* Meals are consumed at fancy restaurants.

✳ Your mom springs out of bed in full makeup with freshly coiffed hair.

✳ Your dad's cheap streak disappears.

✳ The house is spotless and smells of home-baked cookies.

✳ Everyone is nice.

During the early stages of a parent's relationship, the food will always be very good. You will all eat out more often, because restaurants provide "neutral ground." In other words, they think you'll be nicer off your home turf. And you might be if the new sweeties want to explore the trendy little cafés in your neighborhood. And if you can bring yourself to be *really* nice, it doesn't have to end there. You could weasel your way along for some fine meals in pricey places, just by being pleasant company. What better time to refine your palate than at the expense of your smitten father or that guy who keeps trying to impress your mom? Declare lobster season officially open and don't forget to treat yourselves to crème brûlée for dessert. You deserve it for enduring this with a smile.

Chances are pretty good that other booty will roll your way, too. Any number of people may be trying to win that rare prize: a smile from a tense teenager. But get your orders in early, girls, because this careless spending spree won't last forever. Once your parents believe they're "in there" with the new amours, they won't hesitate to tell the waiter just to bring you a hot dog. And sadly, when they declare it's luv, you'll find yourself back at home eating tuna casserole, only New Guy will be at the table too. And if there's a hole in his sock and your mom's legs are hairy again, it's probably serious!

It's Raining Freaks and Weirdos

The princesses Cindy Ella and her annoying sister just couldn't believe their desperate situation. "Jack and Jill are over the hill, so what's the point in all of this madness?" they asked each other. But soon the Queen awoke from her long slumber and began to greet the long succession of emperors in their new clothes who came courting. The sisters sat home on their tuffets eating their curds and drinking nonfat, decaf, iced cappuccinos while their mom *was out at the ball. They would mock the Queen's suitors—all seven of them: Smelly, Greasy, Flabby, Smarmy, Windy, Nerdy, and Slimy. The sisters always marveled at how many men their mother could attract despite that snow white hair of hers. And what was the King's secret? Talk about "playing the field"—he must have dated 101 dull matrons in the last year . . .*

What if you don't like the people your parents are dating? Chances are you won't—not at first, anyway. You probably won't even give them a fair chance, because you're afraid they're trying to take your mother's or father's place at the head of the table. Or worse, that they're going to take *your* place in your parents' hearts. Of course the latter can never happen. However hard that battered old heart may pound in newfound love, your place in it is safe.

Remember, your parents are only *temporarily* insane over their new loves. Think about how you've gone totally nuts over some guy. Did it mean you didn't need your friends or family anymore? Not at all. Although you might have neglected them at first, when he was all you could think about, eventually, you grew more secure and things balanced out. In the same way, the newness of the relationship your mom or dad is having will also wear off, and he or she will get back to "normal." Even if the new person is still on the scene, your parent will once again be the one you knew and loved.

Mind you, it's not unheard of for parents' good judgment to take a mini-vacation when they're fresh out of marriage and still in recovery. This dangerous territory is known as the Rebound Zone. If they make the mistake of getting back into the game too early, boom—into the Zone they go, and there may be some mistakes in their date selection. In fact, they may convince themselves that they're interested in some duds. But if it looks like a dud and smells like a dud, it probably is a dud, and eventually they'll likely recognize it as such. It's better to say nothing to draw the smell to their attention. If you do so, you risk making them more determined to keep the dud around. Besides, you'll gain big points for restraint when they come to the realization themselves. So chill as best you can and let them make their own discoveries. Remember, you want the same privilege of making your own decisions about your dates, no?

Save Your Future

The duds will generally be the exception in your parents' love lives. Usually, they'll hook up with some fairly normal people, and there are plenty of good reasons you should put up with them. First, your parents feel very alone right now and are afraid that will become their permanent status. As gross as it sounds, even parents need a little romance. And you, dears, are no substitute for seeing that wrinkled old face in the next rocker.

Besides, you aren't going to be around the house for that much longer. And believe it or not, somewhere down the road, you'll start worrying about them. Wouldn't it be nice to go about your busy life, knowing they weren't pining alone at home? Eventually, you might need to consider giving the new sweethearts a chance for your own sake. And if they settle down, at least you won't have to endure their dating. Giving your parents a break will avoid the following scenario from ever becoming your reality.

> *There you are, flitting about your apartment, cooking up a killer seduction dinner for that hot new guy from college. You've managed to get rid of your roommate. The place is aglow with soft candlelight, your favorite tunes are on the stereo, and you're looking fine in that new dress. There's a knock at the door. Your heart starts to pound. There he is on your porch looking drop dead sexy and . . .* **OH. MY. GOD!!!!** *Here comes your mother up the stairs behind him with a casserole dish and a video tucked under her arm. "Hi sugar! I just whipped up a batch of sweet and sour meatballs and I can't eat all of them myself, so I thought I'd bring them over. I thought we could eat them and watch a movie . . ." Then she sees him. "Oh my, you have a friend over. Hi there!" She pushes her way past the two of you and is inside your place switching all the lights on. "It's so dark in here, honey, you'll ruin your eyes." Of course you can't turn your mom out now, that would look heartless to your date. So you set another place at the table.*

Is this how you want to end up? Hanging with your mom or dad during the best years of your life? No. And a parent who is happy spending time with a partner is a parent who is not lonely and dropping in on his or her independent daughter, or phoning her constantly with news of coupons for cat chow.

A Change of Pace

. . . Over a few years, things really changed in the lives of our princesses. They now spend half their time living at the stylish loft with their mom and their mom's boyfriend Dopey—who didn't turn out to be much of a prince. Also in residence is Dopey's lazy-ass son, Sleepy. Cindy Ella must share her room with her sister, who had to gives hers to Sleepy.

Their father has taken up with a new love as well, so the girls spend the rest of their time with their Daddy and the Tramp—and her two mean daughters. Her father's place is always a mess, and whenever Cindy Ella is there her evil stepmother is nagging her to clean the place up. The two ugly stepsisters never pitch in and are always raiding Cindy Ella's wardrobe. Why, just the other day she caught the two of them trying to cram their big fat nasty feet into her brand-new clear plastic designer pumps . . .

If your parents do find love again, you may encounter the "blended family." Perhaps you'll soon be living with your siblings, your mom or dad, and a new partner. Maybe their new partners have kids of their own—a situation that can lead to a bad case of Brady Bunch-itis: a piercing pain in the butt as a result of an overly extended family.

If you're the one moving into a new house, it will feel as if you're in alien territory; if the aliens are moving into your house, it will feel like a total invasion of your privacy. Left to your own devices, you might all get used to each other, but you probably won't be left to your own devices. Your parents will be so desperate for peace and happiness in the home, that they will force you together in awkward, overly enthusiastic ways and the results can be disastrous. In fact, nothing can be more off-putting than a parent trying to force your affections. "Honey, say thank you to Carol. Isn't she a fabulous cook?" Or how about, "Aren't you lucky to be sharing a room with someone a year older than you are?

I bet you'll learn a lot from Lisa." (Right. Like how to plan the perfect murder.)

As much as we may joke about these scenarios, we know how stressful these changes to your life must be. You will need to tell yourself constantly that it will get better—and likely faster than you think. But if you feel really depressed about your situation, do not sit around waiting for your worries to fade away. Find someone to talk to about your problems. A good place to start is your school counselor. All you need to do is say you're having some trouble adjusting to changes in your home life, and you'd like some help. A therapist will be able to give you tips on handling things effectively—and your parents don't even have to know you're getting help. You need to do whatever it takes to get though these tough times in one piece.

Take comfort from the fact that things will rarely get this hard again. And remember, we humans are a resilient species and can adapt to almost any situation. One day, you will probably be surprised to find that somewhere along the way when you weren't paying attention, these horrible new "step-people" became your family.

> . . . One day, the princess Cindy Ella was trying to shine up an old lamp her father picked up at a flea market. With a puff of smoke, a genie popped out and granted her three wishes. "Here is my chance to get my old life back," thought Cindy Ella.
>
> "I wish my parents would get back together," she said and— POOF—A strange figure appeared before her eyes. "I'm the ghost of your family's past," he said, and Cindy couldn't help but notice that he looked a lot like her mother's divorce lawyer. The ghost took her back in time and the princess was surprised to see now that things were not as happy as she remembered them to be. In fact, her parents looked angry and miserable.
>
> So the princess made her second wish: "I wish that my parents would at least stay away from these horrible new people in their lives—and POOF—another figure appeared. "I'm the ghost of your family's future," the ghost said, and Cindy thought to herself that this ghost looked a lot like herself, only older and tired. The ghost took Cindy Ella into a future where her parents lived alone in

two small apartments. But wait, someone was knocking at their door! "It's you," said the ghost. You spend every Saturday playing checkers with your father and every Sunday with your mother at bingo." Cindy Ella was deeply troubled: "But what about _my_ life?" "Your life?" the ghost laughed wickedly, "You don't have a life any-more."

The princess quickly made her third wish: "I wish to be young and happy again" and—POOF—she found herself back in the pre-sent surrounded by her parents and their new spouses and their kids. Today is the princess's birthday and she can see how much her family has done to make this day special for her. Even her ugly stepsisters baked her a cake. But most of all, it struck her how happy her parents looked in their new lives. "Make a wish," everyone cried as the cake landed in front of her. "No way," said the princess. "There's no place like home."

And they all lived happily ever after.

part four

Baby, You're
the Greatest

chapter nineteen

Yakkity Yak– Learn to Talk Back

*O*kay, we've spent a lot of time talking about all the supporting actors in your life–your parents, girlfriends, and boys–and it's high time we shifted our focus to the star of the show–you! We know you've probably been struggling to make sense out of chaos lately. Since puberty hit you with a force measuring about 7.5 on the Richter scale, perhaps you've even had moments of feeling possessed by nasty little demons who urge you to follow conflicting impulses. Our goal with the next few chapters is to offer some advice on how to take the challenges in your life in stride. Let's face it, your body is going to change whether you like it or not, so you might as well stretch your mind a little to keep up. Besides, it will give those demons of yours more room to duke it out.

One of the keys to stretching your mind is communication–both with yourself and with others. If you can learn to talk to yourself in a way that silences your inner demons, you'll be able to stop focusing on your weaknesses and tune into your many strengths. It's also important to acquire the ability to communicate well with others so that you can move through life with ease.

The Speed of Sound

We've talked a lot about talking in this book. That's because human culture depends on it. You'll get more out of life if you learn to make it work for you. Maybe your parents complain that it's time you started conversing like an adult. *Excuse me?* You figure you've got *way* too much energy for the vocal stylings of an adult. There are so many thoughts and ideas buzzing around in your mind that when you open your mouth to speak, the words often tumble out at a furious rate. Adults can get whiplash from the speed.

You've probably been managing to get your point across to your peers just fine, but it's important to communicate effectively with people of all ages. It will help you make friends, win over enemies, and achieve some worthwhile goals. If people like you, they'll want to make your life easier. But how can they like you if you don't give them the opportunity to get to know you? You'll need to communicate who you are and what's important to you.

First Impressions

Communication starts before you've even opened your mouth. Never underestimate the power of first impressions; they can make or break a potentially useful new connection. People start assessing you from the moment they see you, so it's important to use the right body language. Are you telling people that you're shy and anxious and lack confidence by slouching and looking at the ground? Stand tall and look them in the eye as if you're proud to be who you are. You should be! You're equal to anyone, so send that message out loud and clear. And flash them a smile while you're at it.

When you're introduced, it's a good idea to say the other person's name out loud to log it into your brain, as in: "Nice to meet you, Bruce." You can do this while you extend your hand. Grasp Bruce's hand *firmly* with strength and self-assurance. A limp handshake is often seen as a sign of weak character.

We know it can be intimidating to meet people outside of your circle of friends. It helps to remind yourself that whether the stranger is your friend's grandmother, a university professor, or the hottest guy in your school, they're all just people like you. Regardless of age or gender, they too start their days with a trip to the bathroom. Just take a few deep breaths and keep in mind that almost every person on this planet loves to talk about himself or herself. Generally speaking, it's pretty easy to get a conversation going simply by asking a few pertinent questions. If you follow that up by listening closely to the response, before long, you'll be off and running.

Lazy Lips

Some people are harder to talk to than others, of course. There are plenty of folks out there who don't do their share of the work. We're not talking about shy people here, but the social lazy asses who love to sit back and enjoy your song-and-dance routine without making the slightest effort to participate. Well, no one is paying you to entertain, so if you've done your best to get a conversation going and you're doing all the work, give it up. Try not saying anything for a minute to see if your new acquaintance will get the idea, but this move can be risky. It takes a lot of confidence to be comfortable with silences. When you're looking into the face of a stranger, it's very easy to give in to the impulse to babble nervously.

Fortunately, most people will meet you halfway by picking up on something you've said and tossing the ball back to you. You can learn to do this too. The key is staying calm enough to pay attention to what the other person is saying so that you can jump on a decent opportunity.

In Search of Common Ground

In your early efforts at chatting, it's better to stick to safe topics. Avoid provocative subjects that may generate plenty of conversation, but not necessarily goodwill (e.g., religion, politics, abortion). You're still trying to cement the first impression you've created, and your goal will generally be to avoid shocking your companion. By the same token, it's a good idea to go easy on the humor. When people don't know you well, they may be taken aback by your jokes. Instead, go heavy on the charm during a first encounter.

Here are a few topics to get the ball rolling: pets, music, travel, the arts, television, film, cooking and food, current events, the Internet, and hobbies. To ease your way into conversation, remember that almost anyone you encounter will:

✳　Want to be liked and respected
✳　Want to be heard
✳　Be a little nervous about opening up to a stranger for fear of judgment
✳　Enjoy discussing his or her interests
✳　Like to laugh and want to be amused

It's usually easy enough to put them at ease by:

✳　Asking open-ended questions that require more than a "yes" or "no" answer (e.g., "How did you get interested in photography?")
✳　Being agreeable
✳　Emphasizing what you have in common
✳　Sparing them the intimate details of your life
✳　Resisting the urge to point out flaws in their thinking

The very best advice we can give you is to become a *generous listener*. Yield the floor with grace and class. Show genuine interest in what people are saying to you, and ask a few relevant questions. Soon they'll be telling others what an amazing conversationalist you are—simply because you got them talking!

The Great Escape

There are no guarantees when you're dealing with other people. You can talk until your tongue bleeds, desperately seeking common ground, only to be met with stony silence or one-word answers. Your best bet in these situations is the slick escape.

There are plenty of good ways to escape a horrendously boring conversation without being rude. At family gatherings, you can slip away to help the host or get a refill of your drink. In the school halls, you can excuse yourself from Mr. or Ms. Snoozefest, by hurrying off to beat the library's closing time, or using the old "meeting a friend" excuse. Whatever reason you use, remember to say "Excuse me, I have to . . ." and make up something plausible and tactful. Telling someone he's boring the crap out of you is not the classiest way to go. Other class-free techniques include:

✳ Checking your watch
✳ Scanning the room for interesting faces or escape routes
✳ Yawning
✳ Whipping out your cell phone to report to a friend how bored you are
✳ Becoming so offensive that he or she turns and runs

Clearly You Lack Clarity

No matter what the audience, you will need to structure your words and sentences to convey your point clearly. Miscommunication can be a dangerous thing. In fact, many a friendship and romance have been crushed under its weight.

Asking someone to relay your feelings to a third person is usually a bad idea. No one else is as interested in your life as you are, so they don't always pay close attention to what you're saying. Also, people have a tendency to select a kernel of truth and embellish it with their own thoughts and words. People have personal biases that you won't know, and even words you plan and say carefully can be twisted to mean something negative. You can never control all the variables, but you can do your best to say exactly what you mean.

Similarly, your best bet for clear communication is face-to-face delivery. Human beings rely on "reading" facial expressions, tone of voice, and gestures to get a full understanding of what someone means. Whether you're offering a compliment or a criticism, the more removed you are from your listener, the greater the chances of being misunderstood. Consider your words carefully when you are not speaking to someone face-to-face. On the phone, you lose two important aspects of communication: facial expressions and body language. E-mail is even worse, because you also lose tone of voice.

That's merely the beginning of the risks attached to communicating "electronically." Going into chatrooms on the Net is like picking up the phone and dialing a stranger's number—or better yet, going to a masquerade ball. People are always bolder when they're wearing a "mask" of anonymity—and that includes you. Even when you actually know the person you're "chatting" with, you can get carried away and say things you wish you hadn't.

I used to chat to my ex-boyfriend a lot on the Net because he lived across the city. One night, we started chatting about sex and we just got braver and braver about what we were saying. I said stuff I never would have told him in person. We ended up breaking up over it because he thought that meant I was ready to have sex with him and I definitely wasn't. The worst thing was that he was so mad that he told all his friends about it. I was really embarrassed.

Make sure your words aren't going to come back to haunt you. The words you send off in haste could be forwarded around the world. And a final word of caution: You don't know that the people in those chatrooms are being honest with you. Is he a 16-year-old cutie or a 40-year-old pervert? No one knows for sure! Someone who knows his way around technology might be able to find out where you live. Don't assume you're totally safe.

Keep at It

Mastering the art of clear communication takes time. You'll become increasingly confident of your ability if you just get out there and yak away. What better time for trial-and-error than now, when people don't expect conversational finesse from you anyway? Some people are born with the gift for gab, but most of us have to practice. It's worth the effort, because speech can be a very powerful thing. Just listen sometime to a coach firing up his or her team so they come back from almost-certain defeat to win the game.

A politician's ability to speak well can move a nation, which is why most of them hire speechwriters to express their ideas eloquently! They can't risk saying the wrong thing, but you can, because the nation isn't listening to your words (yet!). Sometimes you'll put your foot in your mouth, but you probably won't make the same mistake twice. Like anything else, it's a process of continuous improvement. You try something, figure out what worked and what didn't, then try it again a little differently.

Tell It to Your Journal

When you're trying to figure out what you want to say about yourself to the world and how to say it, keeping a journal is a great idea. It's is a safe and legal way of "letting it all hang out." You can free your mind of all the dangerous thoughts that you wouldn't dare share with any other living creature—with the exception of the family dog.

Have you ever walked away from an encounter wishing you'd been more in control of the situation? Well, join the club. In the movies, the characters somehow manage to come out with killer dialogue. In real life, you won't have a talented team of writers to give you clever lines, so it's quite possible you'll fall silent. A journal comes in very handy for reconstructing that event. On its pages, you can become the cool character you want to be instead of the punching bag you felt like. Thinking up all the clever things you *should* have said will help you work out the bad feelings—and prepare for the next time you're ambushed. So give yourself over to the power of the pen!

Hey Diary,

I get to school only to hear that Sean's ex-girlfriend, The Evil Tessa (whose hair looks like a fright wig by the way), is pissed off at me because Sean asked me out. He dumped her a month ago, but she still thinks he like belongs to her or something. Anyway, the rest of the day continued to suck and then after school, Tessa and her stupid gang of she-goons surround me at my locker. I didn't even see them coming (although I felt the force of evil). She leans over my shoulder and whispers, "Stay away from my boyfriend." Her boyfriend!! I was too shocked to say anything—and besides, her friends are really tough. Then she tells me if I don't stay away from Sean, she's going to take me out back and "thump" me.

Man, if only I could live that moment over again. I'd stare her straight in the eye and say, "You listen to me: Sean dumped you for a reason. He likes girls with <u>class</u>. And people with class don't threaten other people. I will go out with <u>whomever</u> I want, <u>whenever</u> I want, and I'm not afraid of anyone who's got to surround herself with her lip gloss gang for protection." I <u>wish</u> I'd said this, but of course I froze. Maybe next time!

The World According to You

Your journal is the perfect place to record your thoughts about the world around you. If you pick up this habit, you'll be keeping company with some great artists, writers, and just plain good observers. Think about Lucy Maud Montgomery, author of *Anne of Green Gables*. As a teenager in the Victorian age, she was discouraged from speaking about her feelings. She turned to her journal as a confidante and nurtured a talent for writing at the same time. If you take a look at her journals, you might find some surprising parallels to your own life.

Few of us will ever have our journals published. Generally, they're meant to be a very private expression of our experiences and feelings. But your journal may become something you can pull out now and again to reflect on your life. Looking back over its pages will bring you perspective and comfort. Sometimes, when you're searching for answers to the great questions of life, you can read over old entries and discover that you don't need to go anywhere for advice. You knew the answers all along. A pen and paper will give you distance and help you get past emotions that cloud your judgment.

Writing about your feelings is therapeutic, because everyone feels unheard sometimes. The people in our lives can be too busy and distracted to lend an ear when we really need one. But your trusty journal will never say, "Can we talk about this later?" It's a very generous and supportive friend.

Your very own "book of truth" can become a written record of your hopes and dreams that will help you figure out what's important to you in life. You can set goals for yourself and measure your progress just by looking

Under Lock and Key

Your journal is for your eyes only. You're allowed to be as petty and mean, or as arrogant and overdramatic as you like. No one is going to edit or judge you. To be sure of that, think about where to keep it. Reading someone else's journal is one of life's great temptations. Do you want someone to peel back your scalp and peer into your naked brain? If not:

1. Disguise the book as something else. Use a school notebook or a photo scrapbook. If funds permit, buy a hardcover ledger or a blank recipe book.
2. Avoid a book with the words my diary emblazoned across the front.
3. Choose your moments to make an entry. It's a private act.
4. Don't leave it lying around in the open, no matter how trustworthy your family is.
5. Rotate your hiding place on a regular basis, or spring for a box with a lock.

back at last year's entries. Sometimes you'll be pleased to see you've come a long way. Other times you'll know you've got some work to do.

When you start to get on in years–say, by age 30–your mind will be so cluttered with the distractions and responsibilities of your adult life that the details of your teen years will start to slip away. Do you want to forget all the special moments you're living now–like the award you just won, the guy you just kissed, the new talent you've discovered? What better way to hold onto your moments of joy than to lock them away in your journal?

Roller Coaster Mama

If your journal is a record of your young life for the "older you" to look back on, make sure you don't horrify your adult self with the discovery that you were a boy-crazy, neurotic, melancholy freak. Sure, you might be any of these things at different times, but that's not *all* you are. Everyone has a tendency to write when overcome by emotion of one extreme or another. That means when you look back you might find your journal is a record of ecstasy and angst—and nothing in between.

Dear Diary,

I hate my life! Nobody loves me. My own family wouldn't notice if the gravitational pull around me suddenly ceased and I shot off into outer space. They'd probably just be glad of the extra room in the house. Five minutes after they learned on the news that I was orbiting Mars, they'd pick out the new wallpaper to turn my bedroom into a den. Even the dog snarled at me today. My friends just tolerate me because they feel sorry for me and Sean hasn't called since our date. Guys suck!

Hey Diary!

It's my birthday today and it was so great! First of all, this morning there was a knock at the front door and when I opened it, my girlfriends were there carrying balloons! They started to sing Happy Birthday at the top of their lungs and all the neighbors kept looking out their windows to see what the racket was about! Next, I aced my geography exam at school, then Tessa got called to the principal's office and finally, Sean was waiting for me at my locker after school with a rose and a teddy bear! He walked me home and kissed me! OH MY GOD— he's the BEST kisser! I can't sleep I'm so happy!

Writing on a more regular basis will give you a more balanced picture of your life than a record of only the victories and defeats. If you're worried about whether you'll have anything to say, here are some ideas to get you started.

✳ Pretend you're chatting to your best friend and tell her about the latest family gossip and what's going on in the world.

* Record your life goals as you see them today. Writing them down is the first step toward achieving them. In fact, try setting goals for the next month or year. Remember, no one is grading you on your effort—except you.
* Daydream about places you'd like to go or people you'd like to meet.
* Include photos or drawings or letters and ticket stubs if you like—anything that helps you describe your life.

Keep it fun. Don't worry about spelling or grammar. Try to find a particular time and place you love to write so that it becomes a ritual. Some people like to write by candlelight, others at a café.

Dear Diary,

Today was just an ordinary day. Looking back over my last few entries, I realize that I could pull this journal out when I'm 40 and think I was a bit of a flake as a teenager. WHICH I AM NOT!!!! I wonder what I'll be like at 30? Maybe I'll be Mrs. Sean Smith, living with my honey on a ranch in Wyoming. I could do online fashion consultation from the ranch! I really like clothes and my friends always ask me for advice and say I have great taste. Who knows, though—I could be doing something I haven't even thought of yet by the time I'm 30. Anyway, I just get so caught up in the ups and downs these days it's really hard to focus. I'm always hungry, my face is breaking out, and I can't get up in the morning. Sometimes I wonder if there is something wrong with me cuz this can't be normal. Can it?

It's normal all right—for now. At this point in your life, you're evolving constantly. This month you're probably a little more sure of your opinions than last month, and you may even be half an inch taller. Why not capture your transformation into adulthood in the pages of your journal?

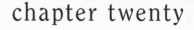

chapter twenty

Hormones:
Your Evil Copilot

Okay, girls, tell us the truth. In the past year, have you . . .

1. Thrown yourself on to your bed so hard in a fit of rage that you nearly cracked your head on the ceiling?
2. Cried uncontrollably for so long that you couldn't remember why you started?
3. Slammed your bedroom door so hard that it came off the hinges and your father threatened to remove it altogether?
4. Stomped into your bedroom to rip all your posters off the wall and break a few things—all while blasting music at full volume?
5. Giggled uncontrollably for so long that you've been asked to leave a classroom, church, or movie theatre?
6. Become pissed off with everyone and everything for no particular reason?

*I*f you answered "yes" to four or more of these questions— Congratulations! You're perfectly normal! If you've answered "yes" to fewer than four, you're either lying to us, or you're repressing so much emotion that you'll explode like a big, ugly bomb one of these days. Perfectly normal, you say? How can such outrageous behavior be considered normal? Well, the important qualifier is that it's perfectly normal *for a teenager.*

Lab Tests Show...

Here's the good news. This behavior, no matter how irrational, is not your fault. There's a sound, scientific explanation. The truth is, you're not the only one controlling your life right now. You've taken on an evil copilot: hormones. Or, as we like to call them, "horror-mones."

We've mentioned these little beasts before, but we've never described how they work. Hormones are natural substances your brain sends to other parts of your body to signal the need for action of some kind. The human body produces hundreds of these hormones, but the one wreaking havoc on your life right now is called FSH, or follicle stimulating hormone. It kicks in when you hit puberty, heading straight for your ovaries, where it causes the egg follicles to trigger yet another hormone called estrogen. Estrogen (which will have you by the throat all your life, we're afraid) then travels throughout your body and causes all those changes you're experiencing, like the sudden appearance of pubic hair and breasts.

Whether we think we're ready or not, hormones make the decision for us about when it's time to start looking like a grownup. What makes it especially frustrating is that while you may look more like an adult, and you may want the adults in your life to stop treating you like a child, you will often still feel like a child inside. Or you may not be too sure what you feel. Emotions have a way of running together when horror-mones are at the wheel.

You'd better hold on to your knickers, girls, because it's going to be a long, bumpy ride. The truth is, you never really get off the hormonal roller coaster. The good days will stretch into weeks and then months. But at the other end of your reproductive years, around age 50, the hormonal decline will be just as brutal. You'll get to watch your mom go through it soon enough. In fact, that's the perfect time to mention any of the grudges you're storing up now!

The Call

Hormones may take over your life so subtly that you're at their mercy before you know what's hit you. By this point, you've probably already noticed a key effect of their influence: a sudden and inexplicable obsession with—you guessed it—boys. There's no point in beating around the bush here. Your hormones have awakened a monster, sexual interest. What you hear ringing through your head is the *Call to Breed*. Now don't be squeamish, girls. It's wonderful nature at work. Your body is merely tuning into the basic human instinct to reproduce.

It breaks our hearts to blast apart your delusions about the myth and mystery of love, but the drive we've mentioned is more elemental than that. It's an extremely powerful force that has helped make the human species the success it is on this planet. But mysterious and romantic it is not. Mixing the *Call* up with romantic notions is a recipe for trouble. We're reminded here of something a woman doctor wrote back in the 1950s, when girls couldn't be as honest about what they're feeling as you can now:

> *"I'm not that kind of girl," they explain to me. This is out-rageous nonsense. Except for a statistical handful who have abnormally low metabolisms, everybody is that kind of girl.*
> —Dr. Marion Hilliard,
> *A Woman Doctor Looks at Love and Life,* 1957

We all hear the *Call,* but fortunately we can choose not to obey it. In fact, obeying it is really the last thing you should do right now. It's a major feat just to make it through the day without blasting into a thousand pieces. Sure, "a basic human drive" sounds like a simple concept, but mastering it is one of the bigger challenges you'll encounter in your lifetime. The human need to eat is also a basic drive, but it's a lot more straightforward: you're hungry, you eat. But just because you hear the *Call to Breed* doesn't mean you should head on out and have sex. You'll hear the *Call* long before your mind and emotions have matured enough to process all the implications of the signals.

Our heartfelt advice is to STOP RIGHT THERE! Stand back, listen to the song your hormones are singing, and wait until your head and heart catch up with your body before taking any action. Then reread the strategies outlined in Part Two and proceed with caution. Don't get too close to those Y chromosomes until you're quite sure you've fully mastered this basic drive. After all, the fact that we can reason with it is what sets us apart from other species.

His Side of the Story

As we've noted, guys hear the *Call* too. In fact, some people say that teenage boys can hear nothing but the *Call*–that it rings so loudly in their heads only really loud music and motors can penetrate the wall of sound. Boys who have survived into adulthood tell us that teenage guys tend to recognize the *Call* for what it is, a sex thing. They're less likely than girls to confuse it with romance.

Teenage boys are rudely awakened from childhood with their first "wet dream," or ejaculation during sleep. They have their own evil copilot at this point, called testosterone. It makes its presence known by deepening the male voice, causing the growth of facial hair, and pro- ducing spontaneous penile erections–even when a guy isn't thinking about anything sexual. Now tell us that isn't a curse!

So, while guys may never admit it, they suffer too. We're not guys so we're biased. We believe they don't suffer quite as keenly under the influence of testosterone as we do with estrogen. But would you ever change places with them? We'll take strapping ourselves into a bra over a sudden, uncontrollable–and visible–erection any day.

Ups and Downs

Hormones can be blamed for a lot, but there's more to the turbulence of adolescence that that. Basically, challenging everything just goes with the territory. As an adult-in-the-making, it is your job to push for independence and question all incoming information. You must challenge the notions that adults have. How better to know what *you* want to believe? The more you challenge, the more you learn. Much as it annoys people–and believe us, it does!–making them defend their point of view is an extremely useful exercise (for both of you–after all, it makes them think too!).

It almost goes without saying that this is a hellish time for your folks. There's no way around it. Remember, until fairly recently you were their sweet, eager to please, little girl. You took their word for things.

And now here you are, questioning every view they hold dear (and many they don't). Then you go on to explain just how they're wrong in the most obnoxious manner imaginable. Oh, don't think we don't know about this. This is what Courtney told us:

> *My dad called me a bitch a couple of months ago. I over-heard him saying to my mother, "Courtney was such a bitch today! I just can't seem to win with her." I couldn't believe it. I was in bed and I cried for three hours. I'd had a really rough day and I thought I could at least expect a little sympathy. But NO!! My mother had bought me this purple sweater and I guess she thought she was being nice—but purple isn't my thing any-more since Debbie started to copy me. I already explained to her that I hate purple now, but she never listens to me. Anyway, I guess I'm yelling a bit, because my dad does the whole 'don't talk to your mother like that' speech—which drives me insane! I'm not even allowed to tell her when she's wrong. They're always trying to control me.*

It took Courtney two weeks to tell her best friend Kelly this story. When she did, Kelly admitted the exact same thing had happened to her. While she and her dad were arguing about some stupid house rules, he'd called *her* a bitch—*right to her face*. The girls admitted they had been hurt—and embarrassed by their fathers' behavior. But then they started to laugh, as they suspected the awful truth: they actually had been bitchy. Both girls admitted it wasn't even the first time they'd been a bit disagreeable.

It takes a big person to admit she's being bitchy. It's called self-knowledge, and like so many things that are good for us, it doesn't come easily. Adults don't always set the best example. You've probably already met a few adults who behave like idiots, but live in complete denial. Some of them may own up to it privately, but don't count on it.

None of this in any way excuses a father from calling his daughter a bitch. There are better ways to express dissatisfaction. But it takes par-ents many years to learn these better ways, and by that point you're usu-ally past pushing the limits. If you're feeling self-aware today, you may just admit that it's fun pushing the limits. In fact, it's an under-appreciated art form. We shouldn't be saying this, of course; but hey, we're not writing this book for parents. There are plenty of insightful books on the market for them. Well, you can make it up to them in your thirties when you need them to baby-sit your own kids.

By then you may have figured out that they were right all along. Maybe not, but that's often the way it works. In the meantime, you must find your own way along the path to independence. And if someone calls you a nasty name now and again, chalk it up to experience. If it's your dad, he'll probably feel quite sick about it when you bring it up in a few years.

Symptoms of Hormonal Overload

Sometimes when your hormones and your need to assert your independence get together—POW!—you're out of control. This generally manifests in those crying jags, giggling fits, and violent rages we mentioned earlier. Let's talk a bit more about the ways hormones torture you and consider some of the ways you can control the damage.

Cry, Baby, Cry

Crying has gotten a bum rap. It's actually a fabulous release for anger, frustration, and sadness. That's why we go to sad movies, even though we know we'll probably fog up the theater.

Some people will tell you that crying is a sign of weakness. We disagree. Think about it. Without this outlet, you girls might either explode or be forced to lower yourselves to other forms of expression such as punching each other out or violent sports, like some other people we know. Crying is emotional detox. It's not always pretty, but it is healthy.

There can be a perverse pleasure to abandoning yourself to a good cry when life seems overwhelming. It's better to indulge the urge privately, of course, so that you can fling yourself dramatically upon the bed. Go ahead and pound the pillow if you want to, and sob loud and long— until you start to hiccup. Take the time to dwell on whatever provoked you, replaying the scene in your mind several times. Wallow in it. You'll know the jag is over when you find yourself on your back wondering what your friends are up to. You'll probably feel the need for a snack, so get up, eat some chocolate, fix your face, and get on with your day.

There are some drawbacks to the crying jag, of course. Once started, it can be hard to stop. And if it happens in public, it's going to be embarrassing later. In our experience, people never forget a jag. They label you as "emotional" forever. This is unfair but it's true. That's why we offer the following tips to help you keep your composure.

When you sense a flood is pending:

❋ Remove yourself from the aggravating situation as quickly as possible.

❋ Get a pal to distract you. DO NOT invite sympathy, which will guarantee waterworks. Instead, get her to talk about anything else—her parents, her dog, her lunch. It will shift your focus from your suffering long enough to recover.

❋ Look up. Believe it or not, rolling your eyes skyward does work. You just have to remember to do it!

❋ Use only the best tissues to mop up a spill to keep your nose from turning into a beacon.

❋ Never cry at night in bed. Tell tale puffiness will be your morning-after reminder of a sorrow long forgotten.

❋ If your eyes become puffy slits, apply cucumber slices or wet teabags for five minutes.

❋ If you've been crying and want to deny it, go for the allergy excuse. People buy this one all the time, unless they use it themselves!

If you've been indulging a super-sob session for too long, give your head a shake. As corny as it sounds, you may be able to snap out of it by counting your blessings and looking around you at those who have bigger problems. It may be hard to remember, at times like these, but there are lots of great things in your life.

A few days after Christy's boyfriend had broken up with her, she was hanging out with some of her girlfriends in her bedroom listening to the radio. "Their song" came on, but before Christy had a chance to get blue, her girlfriends all started singing the song. Badly. In fact, they slaughtered it so thoroughly that Christy could not stop laughing and has never again been reminded of Brian when she hears it. Instead, she is reminded of how great her girlfriends are.

You May Well Laugh

Crying, laughing, laughing, crying . . . One seems to flow seamlessly into the other. The dividing line between emotions is seldom clear, but never is the distinction more blurred than in the teenage years. Hysteria is just part of the package.

Take the laughing fit, for example. It's often a response to an uncomfortable situation, rather than true amusement. And nothing is more likely to make you lose control than knowing you really *shouldn't* laugh. If you're nervous, you may start to giggle. If you're nervous and a guy you like is in the room, consider it a sure thing. If you're nervous, you're in a formal situation, and your friends come around, you may bust a rib.

It's hard to resist the impulse to laugh at certain situations. Say someone passes wind. Frankly, there's no other choice but laughter for girls of any age. One of us had a female boss who farted loudly and frequently, even in business meetings. The only option was to leave the boardroom and fall about the hallway laughing hysterically.

We're not condoning laughing fits in public situations, just acknowledging that they do happen, and that on the wrong day, an all-out giggle-fest can result from next to nothing.

What's more fun than joining a friend in a laughing fit. We hate to discourage them, in fact. They do taper off as the hormonal grip on your neck loosens, but even in university, one of us was asked to leave two classrooms as a result of uncontrollable laughter. There have also been memorable fits at a funeral, in a hospital, and in business meetings.

Here are a few suggestions for minimizing the fallout if you lose control at the wrong time:

* Look away from your friends for five solid minutes—no cheating.
* Pinch yourself as a distraction.

✳ Avoid all food and drink lest you choke or find yourself blowing carbonated pop out your nose (Take our word about how painful this is). This is especially important if there's some hot guy in the room.

✳ Think of serious things like midterms or a touching story about animals.

If you still can't stop, just give into it and get it out of your system. To tell you the truth, most adults find it hard to be tough on a giggling teen, unless they think you're laughing at them. If you are, you'll be in trouble once they clue in, because the madder they get, the funnier it will seem. In that case, expect some yelling and you deserve it. Fortunately that doesn't take the fun out of it. Nor does it mean you will feel sorry about it later. We never have.

The Rage

It's amazing how mad a teenager can get about so little. Some days, just waking up is enough to set you off. This isn't to say that anger isn't entirely justified on some occasions. What's a problem is the high-decibel tantrum of mythic proportions—the ones that drive your parents crazy and make you cringe when you remember them the next day.

It would be nice if we could tell you that it's the logical conclusion of a buildup of small annoyances. The fact is, the tantrum is usually an entirely irrational and largely unpredictable explosion, except for the fact that it's likely to happen at the least appropriate moment. A good example would be the Monday morning tantrum you throw just because there isn't enough Captain Crunch for breakfast. Your mother, who (snidely?) points out that the box of All Bran is still full, must be educated about how important your morning cereal is, especially on Monday. If she makes the mistake of saying anything dismissive, like "Get a grip," it's like fire to gunpowder. After much shouting and slamming of doors, you set off for school hungry and exhausted.

No, it's not logical. And later, it's embarrassing. Fortunately, there are a few things you can do to help.

1. Walk away. If you're ready to boil over, go to another room and listen to tunes, or watch TV. Better yet, call a friend and complain, or go for a walk.
2. Stick to the point. Digressions prolong a fight and make it harder to face up to later.
3. Don't break the sound barrier. No matter what you actually say, if the volume's too high, your point gets lost.
4. Stay so cool that you can remark to your parents that their yelling is upsetting you. Tell them you'll be happy to chat with them when they regain control. (This will drive them insane, which is consolation for not getting to scream yourself.)
5. Save it for another day. Vow to express yourself very clearly in 24 hours, when you've had a chance to think up a good, solid argument. Your chances of winning are better if you're cool and articulate. They're next to nil if you resort to screeching "I hate you."
6. If you have a sneaky feeling you were wrong, apologize. Creative groveling is a good alternative. For example, make your dad some cookies a day or two after calling him an "Overprotective Monster."

The best advice we still give each other when we're angry is to leave it alone. Better to save some face than blow a fit and lose all dignity. Whatever happens, remember that this too shall pass. The people who love you most forgive and forget, just as you will.

The Last Word

Yes, all of this craziness is completely normal. It *will* get better. One day, you'll realize it's been a long time since you lost control. You'll be grateful and sorry at the same time. Sure the lows are a drag, but the highs are amazing! Getting your first job or your first kiss are moments worth getting out of control over. There are long years of boring stability ahead. Enjoy the ride while you can.

chapter twenty-one

It's Your Body, You'd Better Get Used to It

*I*t's a laugh a minute watching your body change, especially when you realize that others (specifically cave boys) are watching it change too. One day you'll be walking down the street quite blind to your burgeoning womanhood, when a car full of guys drives by, windows down: "Nice hooters, baby!"

You'll realize with a sudden shock that you're a child no longer. You now have the dubious honor of being a young woman, the object of far too much interest from the buffoons of the world, and sometimes not enough from the guys you've known all your life. One moment you'll want to cover up in a great big poncho, and the next, you'll be cramming yourself into a tiny Lycra ensemble. You'll be torn between not wanting guys to look at you *that way*, and being compelled to make sure that they do. That's the push/pull of adolescence. You want to show it all off, but only to the *right* eyes. This is challenging, because the guy of your dreams may be surrounded by a hoard of oafs who also admire your new-found assets.

Light Support for Girls

The transformation may begin with your mother's observation that it's time you got your first bra and strapped yourself in for the ride. For many of us, this is a landmark—the first sign that our hormones are starting to sing their song. Some girls are thrilled when they realize what's happening; others are completely miserable. How you feel about the changes your body undergoes is tied very closely to your hopes and fears about whether you'll be attractive to others. It's a sudden self-consciousness that can be overwhelming.

> *I heard my father tell my mother that I needed a bra and I was angry that he noticed it first. I was embarrassed to go to the store with her and humiliated when the clerk walked right into the change room and tried to "adjust" me. I remember I felt like I couldn't breathe in my first bra, and I was so embarrassed that I wore a bulky sweater for weeks after I got it so that no one would notice. Then one day I forgot and took my sweater off and Stephen Simms yelled out in the schoolyard that I was wearing a bra and about 10 guys applauded.*

Here's a voice from the other camp:

> *I couldn't wait to start wearing a bra. All of my friends started to develop early and I was the only one with no boobs. The guys started calling me "Flats." I kept nagging my mom to take me to the store so that I could get a bra but she just said I didn't need one—and that I had plenty of years ahead to wear one. Looking at her depressed me even more because I knew I shouldn't get my hopes up too high: She's an A cup. Finally, my best friend Nikki gave me one of her cast-offs. It was a padded pushup bra. I was so thrilled with my new fake boobs that I bought a new T-shirt to show them off. You should have seen my mother's face when I walked in that night!*

Mirror, Mirror

Once your hormones start working their strange magic, you'll become more aware of your body than you ever were before. Cast your mind back to when you were only seven or eight. How much time did you spend worrying about how you looked then? Did you waste a minute of your day analyzing your body shape or how your face looked? You probably only cared enough about your appearance to want to wear a favorite outfit on special occasions. We'll bet it never occurred to you to slag off your appearance, either. In fact, you were probably more aware of the things that you *liked*—your perfect little nose, your big green eyes, or your long curly hair.

Back in the good old days, you were so busy being you that you didn't take much notice of how you compared to the rest of the girls in the world. Alas, now that you're a teenager and you've plunged headfirst into popular culture, you compare yourself to others endlessly. Everywhere you look there are images of the current definition of perfection and all you can see is where you fall short. You notice that your hair isn't as cool as the hair on those chicks in the MTV videos. And how come you don't have the long, lean body of a supermodel?

How's a girl to deal with such a rude awakening?

Perfect Illusion

Time out for a reality check! First of all, society's notion of feminine beauty changes frequently. In some eras, curves were celebrated. In the '50s, for example, women looked like women. They had hips and breasts and thighs, even bellies. Did you know that one of the greatest sex symbols of all time, Marilyn Monroe, actually wore a size 14? If you don't believe us, rent the movie *Some Like It Hot* and take a good look at Marilyn in her curvaceous glory. Then, in the '60s—the prime of Twiggy—it became fashionable to be rail thin (no hips, and definitely no boobs). A bod like a boy's became what girls craved.

These days, the most desired figure for girls is fit, thin on the bottom half and "stacked" on top. Well, with few exceptions, that's simply unattainable. We're built to breed, girls, and that means having hips. Besides, those who reach the exalted C-cup status usually make it there because they also have some padding on the hips and butt as well. Meanwhile, the girls who are naturally skinny tend to be AA.

We know that a dozen celebrities will come to mind whose figures prove us wrong here. Well, don't be fooled by celebrity bods. They are the exception to the rules of nature. A few women manage to walk away from the body lottery with thin hips and big breasts. Most of the people you see on TV and in the movies were lucky to be born the cutest of the cute. They are not, by any stroke of the imagination, *average*. And keep in mind that what they weren't born with, they have the money to buy. Many celebrities turn to plastic surgery to attain the current beauty ideal—with breast implants, nose jobs, or liposuction.

When you find yourself consumed by envy for the so-called perfect bodies in TV land, remind yourself that it's their *job* to look that way, and it can take hard work. Celebrities have the time and the coin to spend on personal trainers. You'd look buff too with the help of a full-time professional, not to mention a chef at home to make your nonfat gourmet meals. The "stars" are under constant pressure to starve themselves. It's not enough to have talent or skill in La La Land, you need the "six pack," too. How would you like it if someone—make that a vast audience—were continually monitoring your weight? You'd be trading in your birthday cake for a celery stick and enjoying a spinach and wheatgrass shake every day for lunch. Are your mouths watering yet? Don't worry, you'd get a mouthful or two of lean protein (egg whites are delicious!) to fuel you up for your two-hour workout.

What hard work and denial can't do, airbrushing can. The face you see on the cover of a glossy magazine has been touched up a lot. With the help of a post–photo production team, anyone can look fabulous. Arms and thighs can be smoothed out, lengthened, and thinned down. Tiny wrinkles and blemishes can disappear altogether.

How horrible for the rest of us, who have to make do with what nature gave us (along with a tube of coverup cream)!

A Nose Is Just a Nose

Here in the real world, all girls can be beautiful because of *who* they are and how they feel about themselves. Very few people are lucky enough to have every feature turn out to be beautiful. Most of us have lots of average features offset by a few standouts. In the end, this makes for a much more interesting face. And believe it or not, interesting is more attractive than perfect. As a matter of fact, perfection is boring.

Wouldn't life be dull if you looked around on the street and saw hundreds of identical Barbie and Ken clones?

Okay, so maybe you're thinking that you could live with the boredom of seeing perfection staring back from the mirror day after day. Well, what would make you happy? How about a smaller nose, thinner thighs, bigger boobs—all the beauty money can buy? Would that *really* make you happy? It might help, but only because it would make you feel more confident about yourself, and that in turn would give you courage to pursue your dreams in life. The nose job won't land you the best guy, the best education, or the best job in the land. Regardless of your schnozz, you'll be the same person on the inside, and it's what goes on in there that truly affects your chances of success.

Whether you've got a pert little nose or a sizable honker, you'll face the same stumbling blocks. What you can achieve with a perfect snout, you can achieve with the snout you were born with. Your personality won't change just because your face or figure does. Success is still at your fingertips. For example, your talent for dancing won't be overshadowed by your nose—unless it's so big it knocks you right off balance!

The Chameleon

Girls of all ages are guilty of trying to alter their appearance to please others. That's such a waste of time and energy! It's so much easier just to please yourself and let others think what they will. Besides, the best way to please others is to love the person you already are.

Take a look around school. Who are the most popular kids? Are all of them perfect? There are always a few gorgeous people who are popular because of the way they look, but often the average people with the great personalities have the most confidence, charisma, and overall appeal. The kids who focus on enjoying life instead of worrying about their looks are the ones who are the most fun to have around.

It's not that we don't understand how anxious you are about your appearance. Believe us, we do. One of us likes her legs and dislikes her nose. The other likes her nose and dislikes her legs. Our beliefs about these features haven't affected our careers, love lives, or overall happiness—but they do make us a well balanced writing team!

Very few women are happy with the entire package. Your confidence will be much stronger if you develop your other qualities, like your sense of humor. After all, if your popularity rests on a "nice ass" or a "great rack," you won't know what to do with yourself when these features go where gravity always takes them—*down*.

But hey, if obsessing over your looks by working out three times a day and watching every bite you put into your mouth sounds to you like a life lived to the fullest, you're welcome to it. Just don't coming whining to us in 20 years when you leave the gym one day and discover life has passed you by. You don't want your only claim to fame to be that you still fit into a size 4 dress, do you? Where's the balance?

By then, society's ideal of beauty might have shot up to a size 14 again anyway, and you'll be on the fringe. That ideal can be expected to change often enough to keep the beauty and fashion industry booming. Meanwhile, you're stuck with the body you have and its basic configuration will never really change. If you are pear-shaped, you can be a bigger pear or a smaller pear, but a pear you will be. All the dieting and training in the world will not change that. So what are you going to do? Spend your whole life unhappy while you attempt to morph into something that's unnatural for you? Why not just relax and be the best size 4 or 16, short or tall, skinny or curvy girl you can be? You can't trade it in for a different model, so you might as well accept what you've got. If you're always fighting nature, your unhappiness will show on your face, and that's about as unattractive as it gets!

Because You're Worth It

So what if you don't have the fullest lips or the sexiest eyes on the block? Instead, you may have great legs, a perky butt, or beautiful hair. Everyone has a few really great features. Identify yours, play them up, and feel good about looking your best. Have some fun by experimenting with different haircuts and colors, makeup, even tattoos or piercings. Mind you, with these last two, you might want to go the temporary route first. Before you get ink done, take a moment to visualize a butterfly on your butt cheek when you are 60-something and it's sagging. It won't be such a pretty picture then!

While you're learning to love and respect the body you've got, you might as well learn how to take proper care of it. Good nutrition will fuel a healthy body and help keep your skin beautiful. If you don't want to end up looking like a prune in 15 years, slap on that sunscreen and throw the smokes in the trashcan.

If you think you're consuming too many calories, find an exercise you enjoy and get your body moving. It's a great way to burn the fat and clear the mind. In fact, now is the best time to start working out on a regular basis. Good fitness habits during your teen years will help you maintain a slim, healthy body all your life.

The moral of the story is moderation. No single thing—be it smoking, food, drink, drugs, or sex—should rule your life. Don't give control of yourself over to anyone or anything.

If you feel that your worries about your weight and appearance are getting out of hand, talk to someone about them right away. The longer you wait, the greater the damage to your self-esteem, not to mention your body, will be. This problem is very common and help is close at hand. Start by contacting your family doctor or the school nurse. You won't be the first one who's talked to them, and they won't make you feel embarrassed about how you feel. In the meantime, here are some excellent Web sites you can check out, and some numbers to call for help, free of charge:

www.something-fishy.org
www.eating-disorders.com
Eating Disorders Awareness and Prevention (EDAP) 1-800-931-2237
    (in the U.S. only)
The Renfrew Center 1-800-REN-FREW
Rader Programs 1-800-841-1515

You owe it to yourself to take good care of the only bod you're going to get. Do your best to tune out the opinions of the rest of the world. We know it's tough to ignore the judgments of others, especially when they're coming from attractive males. A guy we know once made this remark about a female fitness instructor who could have run his sorry butt into the ground: "She's in good shape, but she's not shaped good." Sadly, he was born into the age of *Baywatch,* and for a while he believed that what he saw on TV is possible for all to attain. Fortunately, no self-respecting cave boy turns away women who look healthy. Our pal was no exception: he married a full-figured girl!

In the end, you have to feel good about what you've been blessed with and to hell with the rest of 'em! Perhaps our old college cheer can sum things up here:

> *We don't give a damn for any old man,*
> *who don't give a damn for us!!!*

chapter twenty-two

Help! Who Am I?

Good afternoon, ladies and gentlemen, and welcome to Whose Life Is It Anyway! *Today, our contestants will be battling their families and each other as they try to figure out who they are and what the hell they are meant to do with their lives. They'll be competing to win a lifetime supply of happiness—and a lucky few will go on to compete for fame and fortune. So stay tuned because you won't want to miss a minute of the gut-wrenching drama as our players' lives unfold before your very eyes.*

Maybe you've noticed (unless you've been snoozing for the last 14 years or so) that it's a big world out there. And although it's exciting to explore it, trying to figure out exactly where you fit into the big picture can be overwhelming. It's enough to make you throw your fate into the hands of a game show host. After all, everyone wins something on those shows, even if it's just a lifetime supply of baked beans. That's not so bad compared to what might happen in real life if you make a bunch of bad decisions and have only yourself to blame.

Right now, your head is probably full of questions:

Who will I be going out with next Saturday?
What is the chemical content of a Twinkie's cream filling?
Where will I find a really funky pair of red boots?
When will my parents realize I deserve my own phone line?

Why did I ever think "going commando" was a good idea? (Always wear underwear when the wind and the skirt are high!)

No! Not those questions. *These* questions:

Who am I?
What am I destined to do with my life?
Where am I going?
When will I get there?
Why did I ever think "going commando" was a good idea? (Some questions keep coming back to haunt you!)

With a body that's changing faster than a rocket leaving the earth's atmosphere, you're bound to feel minor anxiety or maybe even massive panic. Once you've got the outward appearance of an adult, it's easy to feel pressured to live up to the responsibility of owning it. Meanwhile, you're trying to sort out who you really are from what others want you to be.

Pressure, Pressure, Pressure

This is an important time in your life. You need to sift through a lot of information—and misinformation—to decide what is right for you. You're probably feeling the heat from your peers to move into new territory. But it's up to you to figure out if you want to explore it. Mind you, these are not decisions you need to make in a vacuum. It's always best to talk to people with more life experience about directions you consider pursuing. Parents are usually open to these discussions but if you don't feel comfortable talking to them, seek out an older friend or relative, or a guidance counselor.

Equally important, you need to start looking *inside* to make sure you're staying true to yourself. You may not realize it, but you already have a strong personal "code" of behavior that defines you. It has grown out of your relationship with your family and friends and your experiences at school and beyond. Your personal code is the one thing that sets you apart from everyone else you know and allows you to make statements like "No, I wouldn't feel right about doing that." The more you stay true to your personal code by doing only what you're truly comfortable doing, the happier you'll be—and the more you'll achieve in life. It will give you a framework for everything you do and something to measure your progress against as the years roll by.

During the teen years, it's easy to slip into the limiting habit of worrying less about what makes *you* happy and more about what makes *others* happy. This affects even the simplest decisions:

> *When I was little, I had long hair until the day I saw this figure skater on TV. She had this really cool short haircut. I asked my mom to take me to the hairdresser so I could have mine cut the same way. I loved it and kept it short for years. But now that I'm older I wear it long again because guys always go on about how they prefer girls to have long hair. So even though I really want to cut it again, I leave it long.*

Because you're faced with many pressures and competing demands, you may neglect to figure out what really makes you happy. Or perhaps, like many people (women especially), you don't even think you have the right to be happy. You may think you need to earn it somehow by being good enough, or smart enough, or nice enough. There's one message we want to give you loud and clear in this book: *Every last one of you deserves to be happy.* Actually, you have an obligation to yourself and to the people who love you to try to find happiness. Mind you, searching out the exact thing that makes you happy can be a challenge, but it's also a lot of fun!

The key to accepting that you deserve to be happy is confidence, and this is hard to come by for many girls. In fact, women are known for becoming their own worst critics, which is a shame. Think for a moment of how generous and forgiving you are with your friends. You allow them to make endless mistakes and support all their efforts to try again, don't you? Well, how about giving yourself the same freedom? Allow yourself to try new things and expect that you won't be perfect the first time out. Set some manageable goals and watch how your confidence grows as you achieve them. Take baby steps toward your big dreams.

Sure, it will take awhile to get there, but you'll get stronger and stronger with every small triumph.

In your quest for self-confidence, be careful not to expect someone else to deliver it to you all nicely gift-wrapped, especially a boy. This is something only you can give yourself. Having a boyfriend can be a blast, but all the guy can do is *add* to the happiness you've already found. If it's not there in you, he won't be able to conjure it up for you. Besides, it's a mistake to give someone else that much power over your life and happiness—or the burden of such great expectations.

Sex and Drugs and Alcohol

While it's never been easy for teens to say no to what their peers are trying, these days it's harder than ever. We're all inundated with images on TV, in advertising, in movies, and in music videos that suggest everyone is into sex, drugs, and booze. It's just a non-stop party in the sophisticated world we live in. The modern teen can't be hip unless she gets out there and gets down, right?

Well, no question, some teens somewhere are definitely indulging in drugs and alcohol, but not nearly as many as you'd think. Remember, the role of the media is *to sell*—to sell a product, and to sell a lifestyle that supports that product. To keep our balance today, we all need to be critical of what we see and hear. That means never taking any message from any source at face value. Question everything! Okay, so you don't always need to do it out loud (your friends will find it annoying), but get into the habit of silently assessing whatever you see and hear. Then compare these messages to the personal "code" we mentioned earlier.

That's what you need to do whenever you're encouraged to try something you're not sure about. Weigh your decision very carefully against the "code." Is starting to drink consistent with who you think you are, who you want to become, and what you want to achieve in life? Do you want to lose control? Remember that with any of these things— especially drugs and alcohol—it is very easy to cross the line and lose control. It's a slippery slope. One day you're having a single beer, and the next it's a few more. When it gets to the "few more" stage, it's going to affect your performance in every aspect of your life, and that may well sabotage your hopes of reaching your goals.

Generally, if you really listen to yourself, you'll find you don't really want to lose control. After all, you're already trying to wrestle control of your life out of your parents' hands. Don't you want to hold onto it yourself? Why give any of your hard-won personal power over to anyone or anything else?

Maturity means thinking things through from every angle. It means weighing the consequences and refusing to follow the crowd just for the sake of following the crowd. Saying yes is easy. It takes a lot more courage to say no to things that don't make sense to you. We can't deny it's the harder choice, but we *can* tell you that you won't ever regret taking the time to consider a decision carefully.

Sometimes you'll hear a lot of bleating from the herd of sheep. They're mindlessly following the flock and urging you to slip into your woolly coat and join them. Well, tune them out. There's nothing wrong with being an independent sheep—or better yet, the shepherd. In other words, don't let your peers drag you down. If your decisions feel right to you—if they're consistent with your "code"—then do your best to ignore the critics. Keep in mind that "no one can make you feel inferior without your consent."

Role Models

Other people can be very helpful in figuring out life's big picture. These mentors and role models will have the traits you admire and aspire to have yourself and will often have reached goals similar to the ones that you're setting.

If you don't think you have any role models in your life, think harder. They're everywhere—at school, on TV, in books. A role model doesn't have to be *everything* you hope to be. Different people can model different talents, values, or skills. Maybe your aunt is a fabulous communicator or your friend's mom is a natural actress. These are people you may want to take the time to study. Some role models are even closer to home, maybe even inside it! Sure your parents drive you crazy, but you might just find they have some abilities or character strengths you're secretly proud of and want to emulate. (You're probably unknowingly copying some now!)

It's always fun to ask other people about who has influenced them in life. The answers may surprise you.

My granddad was only 15 when he joined the Second World War. He was signed on in the special services branch and was sent over as a civilian (which means out of uniform) to enemy countries to sabotage their communications systems. His contact in several of these places was a 20-year-old woman named Margaret, who lived among the enemies as a local. She risked her life every day to help her country and she helped my granddad escape from more than one prison camp. He says he would not be alive today if it weren't for her help. He really admired her courage. She died in a plane crash soon after the war ended, so my granddad has kept the image of a 20-year-old girl as one of his role models all of his life.

Take a minute to think about who inspires you most in life. Identifying what it is you admire about them will help you figure out the qualities that you'd like to develop. If you know the people, don't be shy about asking for advice. Most people will be pleased and flattered, and delighted to share with you any knowledge they have that could help you reach your goals.

Follow Your Heart (or Should We Say, Your Gut?)

The last thing we want to say to you is that however tempting it may be, resist the urge to disguise or change who you are or what you believe to fit in with others. Better to find people to hang with who will accept you as you are. There isn't much to be gained by hanging around people whose minds are so small they only accept people who are exactly the same. The people most worth impressing usually dance to their own tune anyway. Just look at any great artist or musician and you'll find he or she probably didn't follow the herd.

If you want to try something new, try it—even if your current group of friends thinks it's hugely uncool. Trends change. What's considered lame now may well be the coolest thing going in five years. When we were in high school, for example, anyone who played the accordion or fiddle would have been considered far from hip. Today, it's cool to play these instruments in a band. Who knew?

You've probably heard it before, but it bears repeating: "Life is not a dress rehearsal." This just means you've got to get out there and do whatever you want to do now—not later, when it becomes trendy, or you lose weight, or your friends support your choice. The day may never arrive when all the stars are perfectly aligned for you to start scuba diving or rapping. Do it NOW or regret it later, when it's too late to catch up.

Managing your life is ultimately your responsibility, and your teen years do not have to be like a ride on a runaway train. You can climb up behind the controls and take charge. Make decisions that will benefit you in life. If you're tempted to do something that could sabotage your success, *don't*. It's that simple. You've got the power. Use it.

Sure, it takes some effort. In an ideal world, we could sit back and let someone else drive and always be thrilled by our route and destination. The reality is, you've got to learn to drive yourself and stand behind the decisions you make about direction and speed. Keep in mind that the decisions you're making about your ride now will influence you all your life, but you'll also be able to take full credit if the scenery is great. We wish you a pleasant trip!

And that's it for today's episode of Whose Life Is It Anyway! *Our winner is the girl with the self-respect, ladies and gentlemen. Some people call that "attitude," but it's clear she just knows what she wants and she's willing to do what it takes to get it. That's what makes her a winner! We'll have her back for tomorrow's show, but I'm not sure we're going to be able to stump her—she seems to be ready for anything. Let's give her a big round of applause!*

Index